BRIAN RALPH.

MISTER SNOW-BOY
WARREN CRACHEAd.

BABY ROBOT
JAMES KOCHALKA SUPERSTAR.

VIOLET
IAN LYNAM AND SIMON GANE.

THE TWINS AT SUMMER CAM
JENNY ZERVAKIS

THE POWER OF LOVE
PETE SICKMAN-GARNER.

LAND OF PROMISE
JEFF ZENICK.

THE SWEETIE
RIBS!

FRIENDS AND FAMILY
MATT MADDEN.

ШЕЛФ

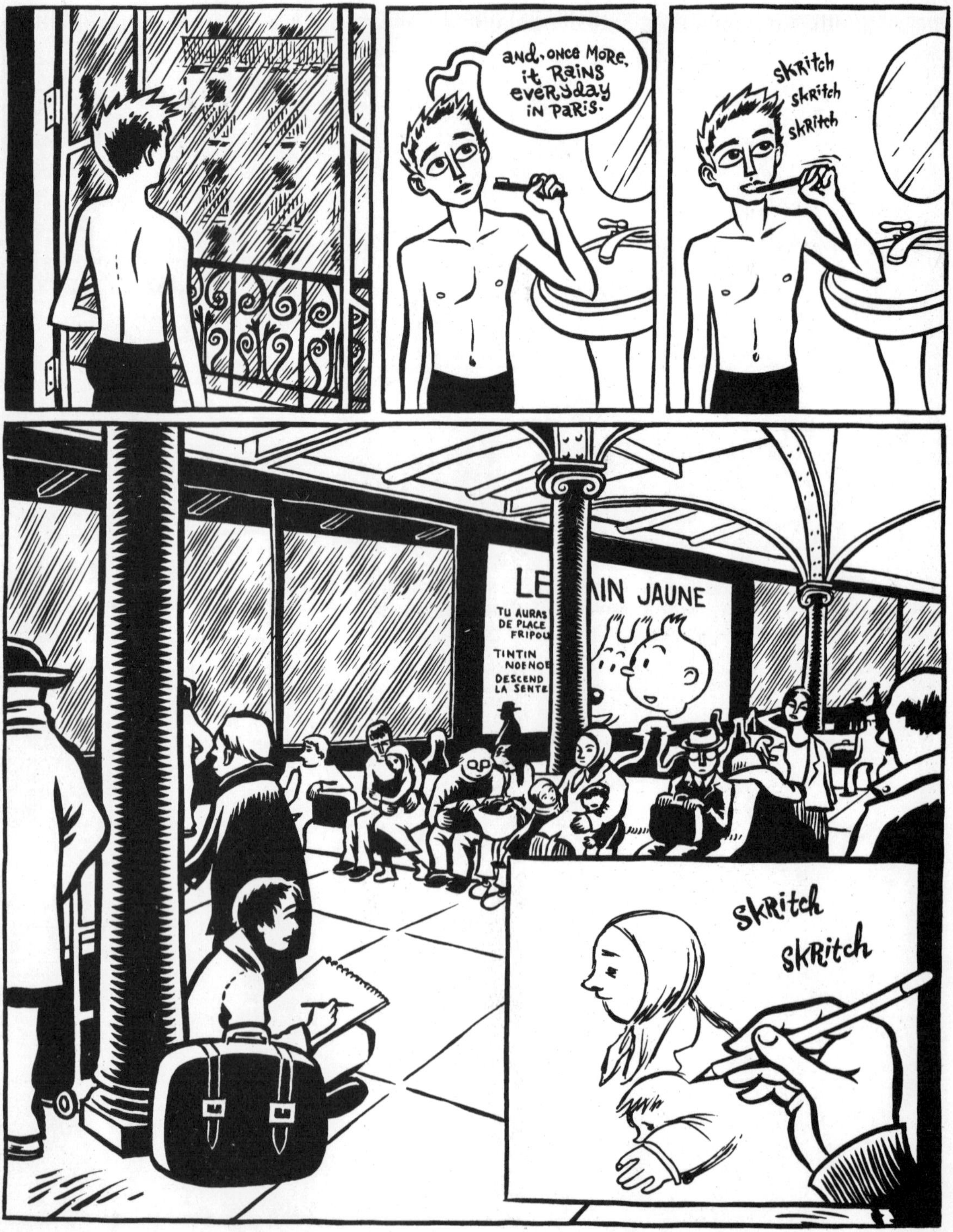
and, once more, it rains everyday in paris.
skritch skritch skritch
LE
AIN JAUNE
TU AURAS
DE PLACE
FRIPOU
TINTIN
NOENOE
DESCEND
LA SENTE
skritch skritch

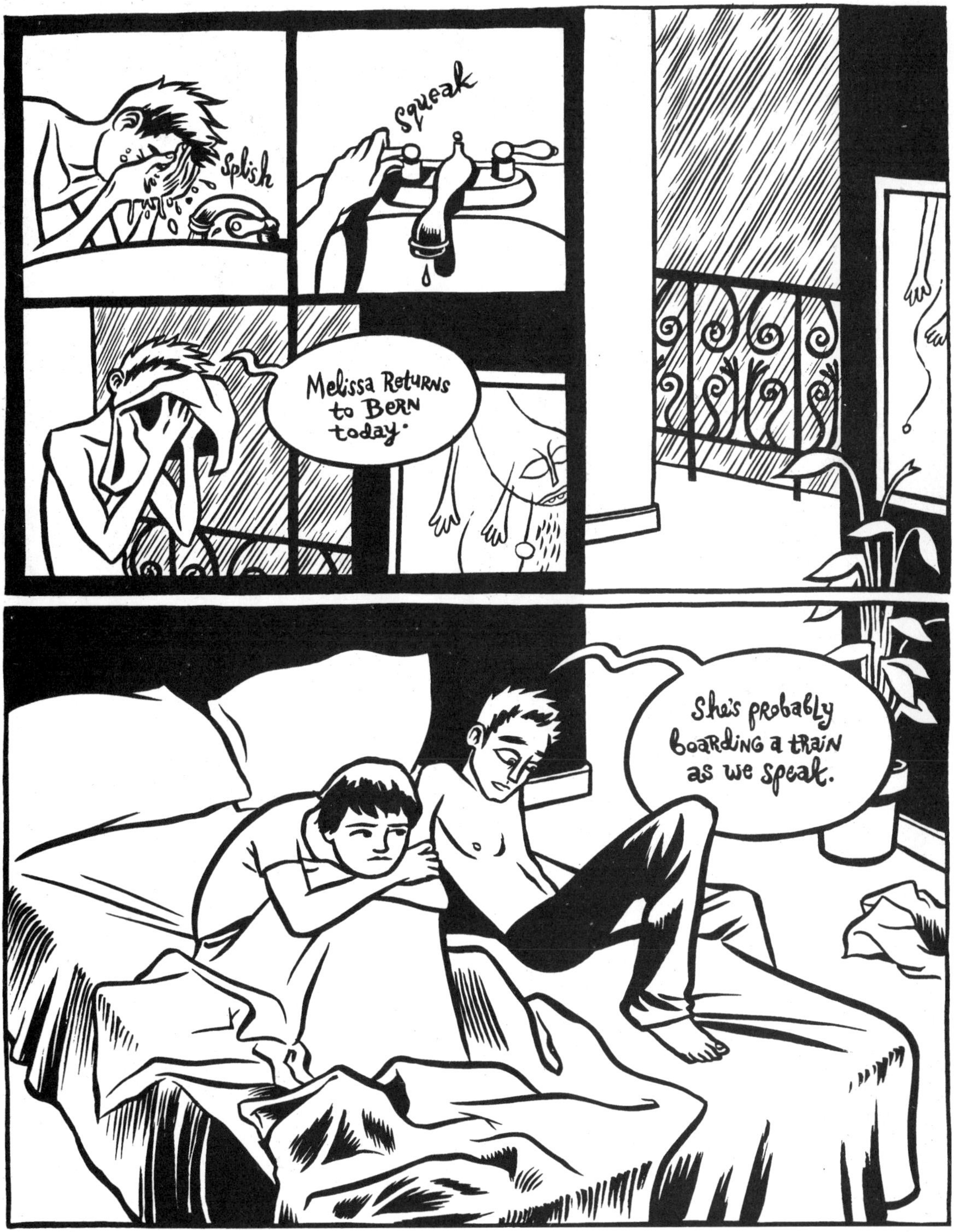
Splish
Squeak
Melissa Returns to Bern today.
She's probably boarding a train as we speak.

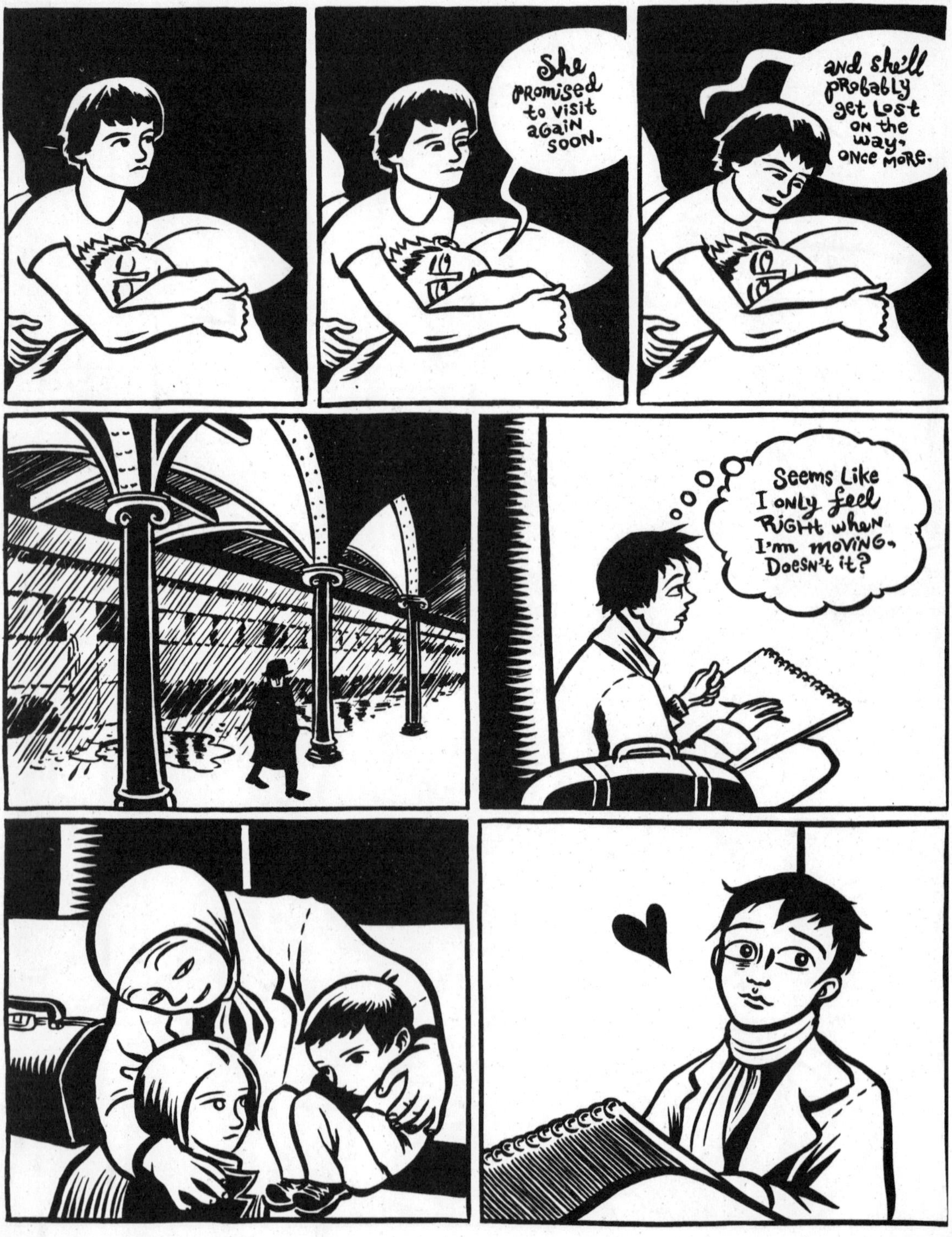
She promised to visit again soon.
and she'll probably get lost on the way, once more.
Seems like I only feel right when I'm moving, doesn't it?

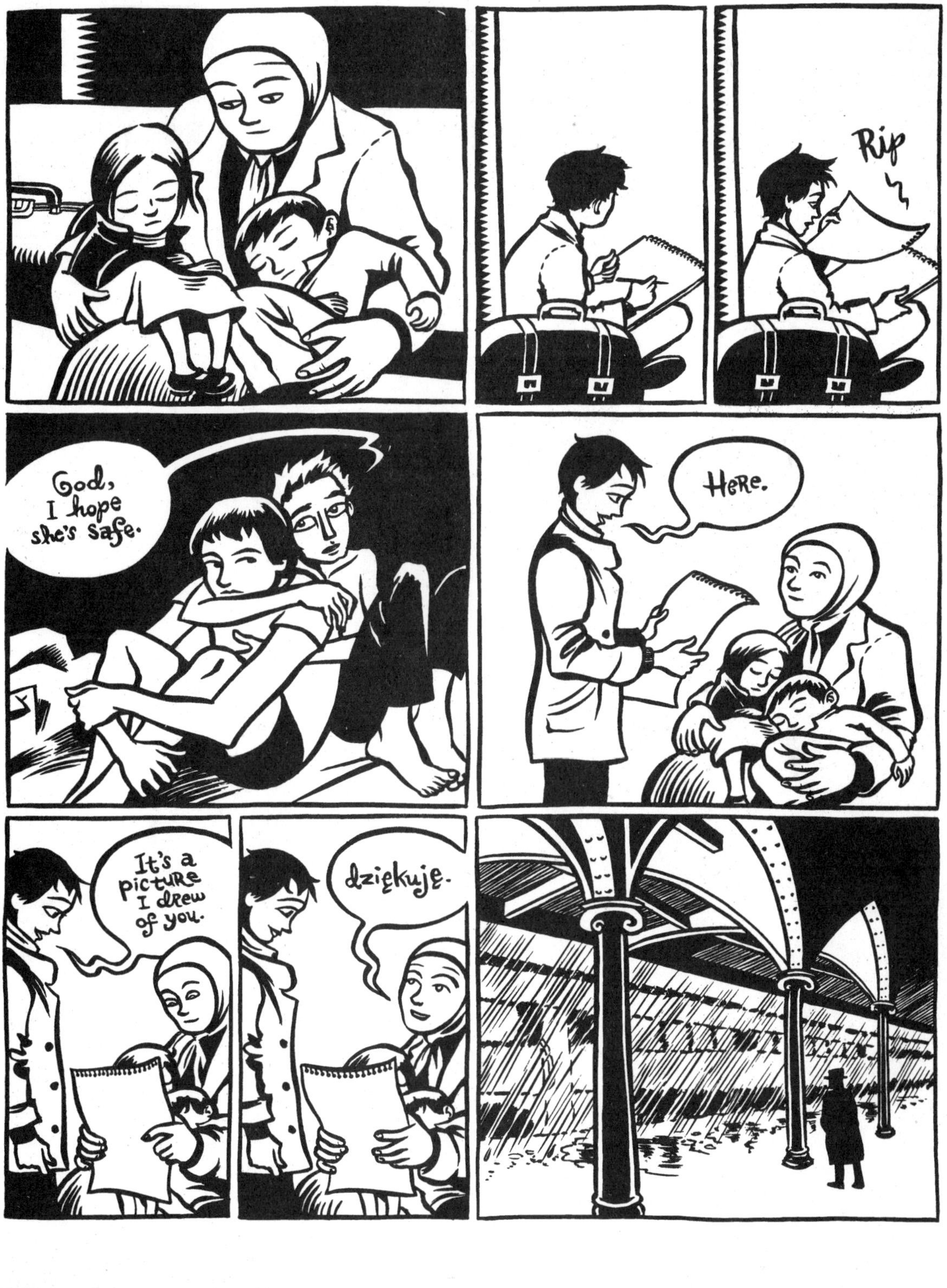
Rip
God, I hope she's safe.
Here.
It's a picture I drew of you.
dziękuję.

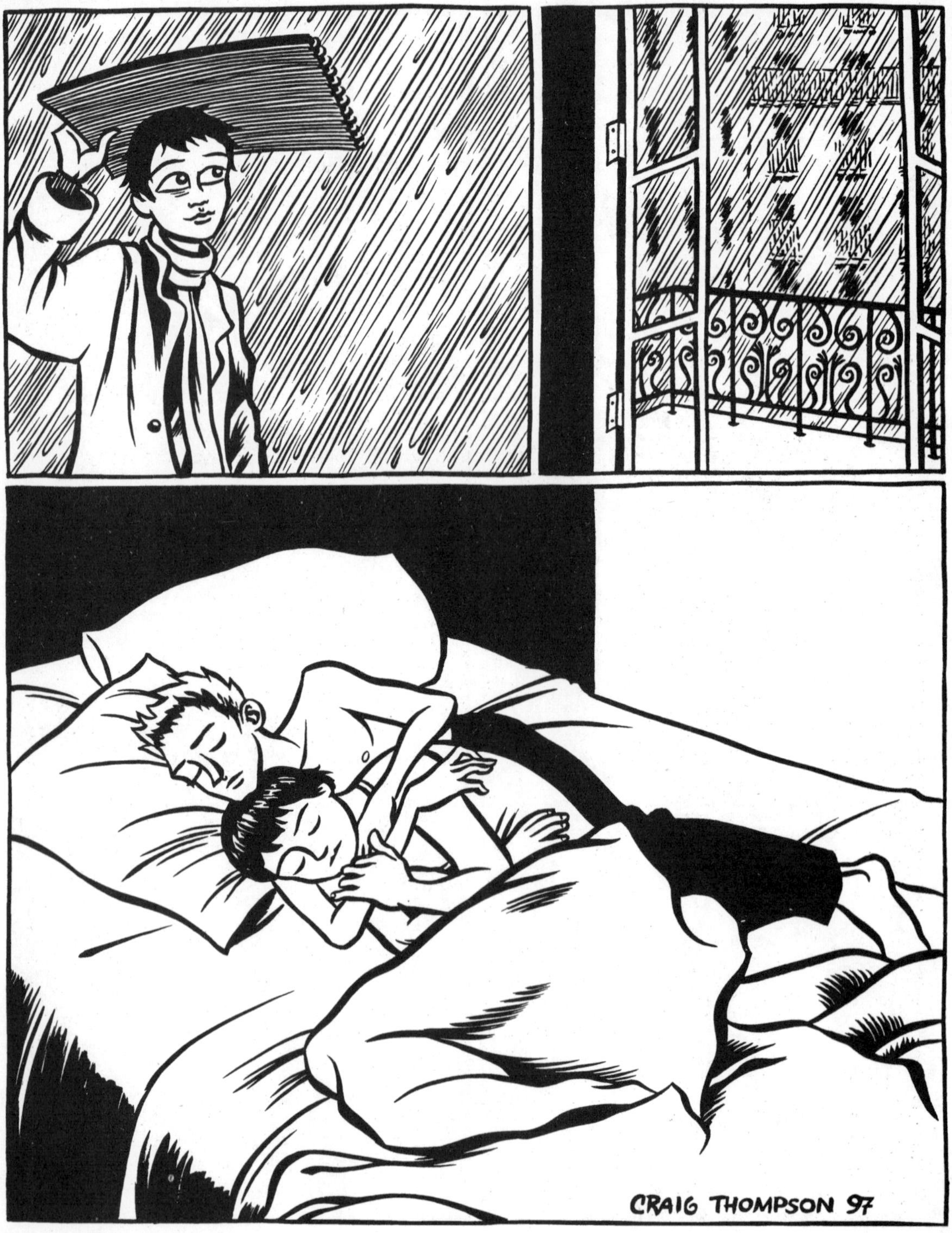
CRAIG THOMPSON 97

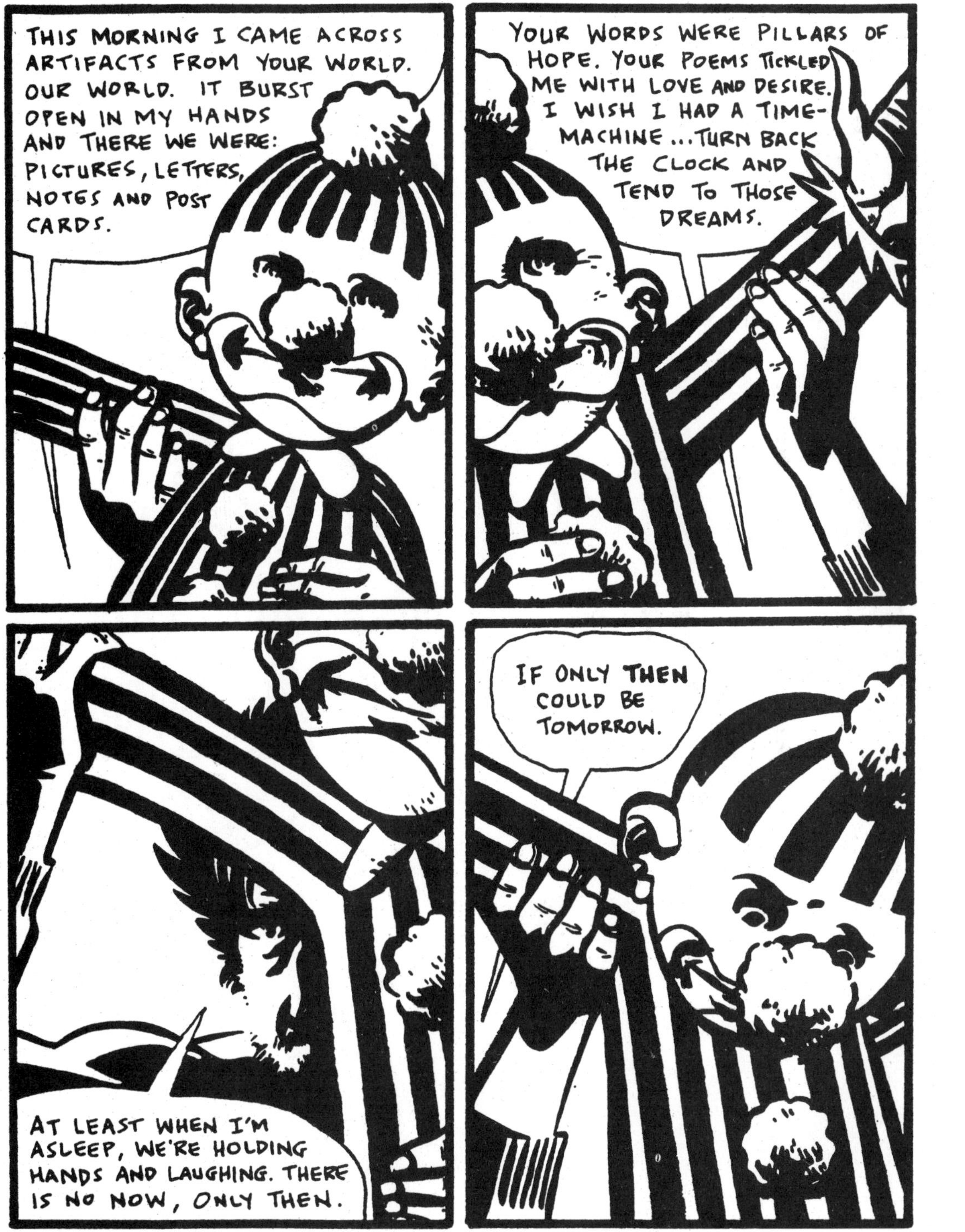
THIS MORNING I CAME ACROSS ARTIFACTS FROM YOUR WORLD. OUR WORLD. IT BURST OPEN IN MY HANDS AND THERE WE WERE: PICTURES, LETTERS, NOTES AND POST CARDS.
YOUR WORDS WERE PILLARS OF HOPE. YOUR POEMS TICKLED ME WITH LOVE AND DESIRE. I WISH I HAD A TIME-MACHINE... TURN BACK THE CLOCK AND TEND TO THOSE DREAMS.
AT LEAST WHEN I'M ASLEEP, WE'RE HOLDING HANDS AND LAUGHING. THERE IS NO NOW, ONLY THEN.
IF ONLY THEN COULD BE TOMORROW.

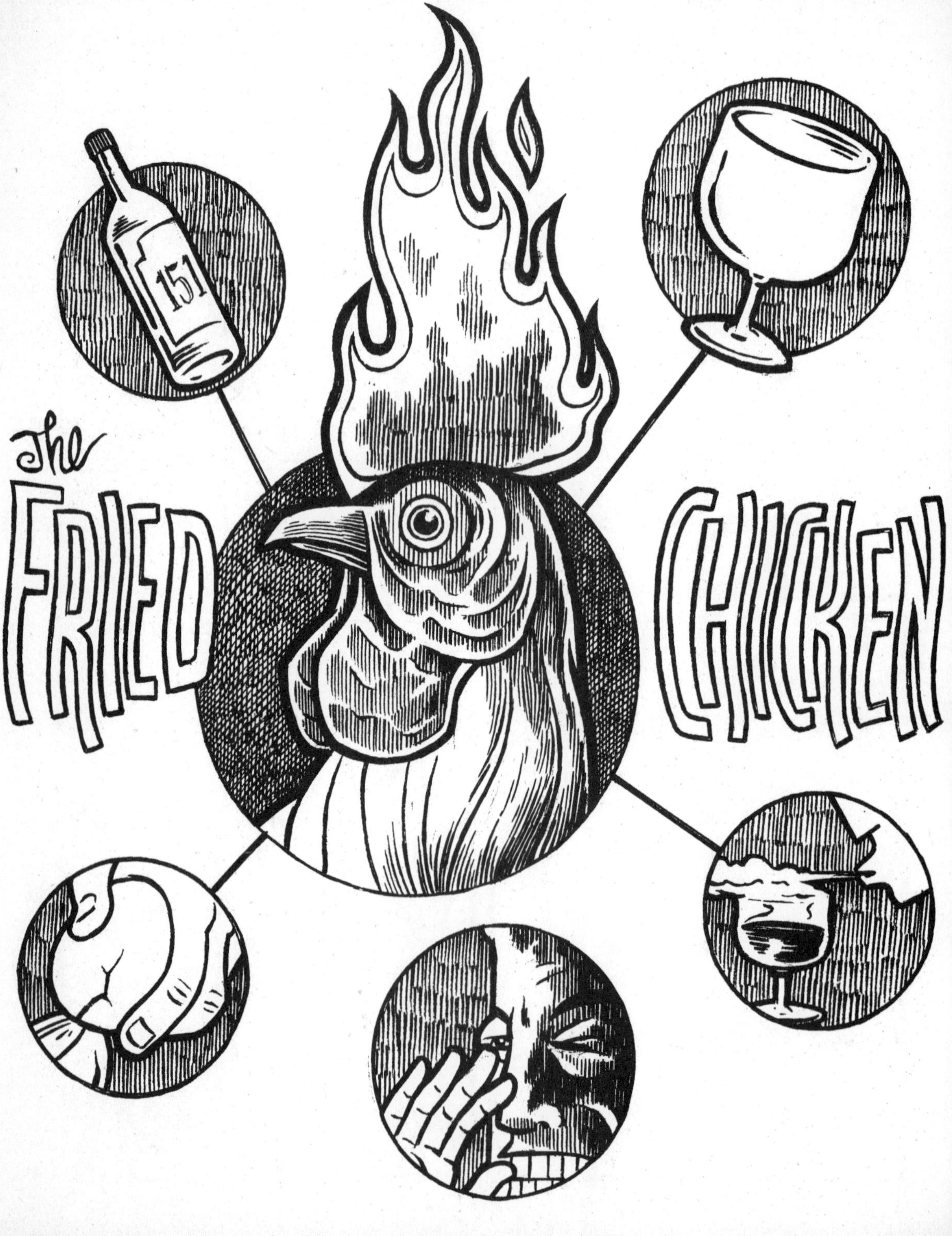
The
FRIED
CHICKEN
151

COCKTAIL COMICS IN THE CITY OF ROSES

by C.K. Lichenstein

Your bartender tonight is serving a new drink this Happy Hour called Oni Press and is bringing back a local, favorite special, the *Rust City Annual.* Both made their premiers at July's San Diego Comic Con, Oni going so far as to have a smashing hotel party, complete with plenty of GOOD, free booze, and was the buzz of the con. So, don't mind the full ashtrays or the drunk in the corner and we'll see about getting you home safe and sound and just a little buzzed.

Rust City #3 is an anthology of "Portland underground comix" talent. This thick 164 page tome is swirled with diversity and talent. Some favorite highlights are the concluding 7 installments of Discography by Rust City founding member Steve Hess. The series of one page strips record the oft humorous and insightful road of Hess and his musical upbringing, from 80's pop drek, to Alice Cooper, to the myriad of bands invading the alternative scene today. Amy Sacks, also a founding member, contributes more of her lyrical and almost whimsical strips that have appeared in local rag Anodyne. The third founding member, Spider Moccasin, took over the editor's reigns this issue producing *Rust City's* best issue to date. His article on Portland's own Pander Brothers focused on the duo's growing works in the comics field and gave an insightful local view. Spider's auto-bio text piece *"The Politics of Cartooning"* focused on his growth towards his identity as an artist and a Native American in an ambivalent Portland scene. Also at the bar were Ian and Ty Smith's (of *Odd Adventure Zine*) silent and stylishly rendered warning about the dangers of a space vegetable, a cut and copy flip book by animator Webster Colcord and a new, cutesy tale of Suzy Q by animator Robin Ator, that combines The Little Mermaid with the feel of a Tex Avery cartoon. I do not have time to mention them all nor did I truly enjoy all the stories, but I think the different approaches to the medium give plenty for readers to latch onto. (PO Box 25476, Portland, OR, 97298)

On December 19th, 1997, this author and Mssr. Warnock, we're invited to Berbati's (a favorite local hangout that is part Greek Restaurant, part hipster bar) for beer, Bavarian Mudslides and the release of *Bad Boy*, the first comic from Oni Press. Publishers Bob Schreck (late of Dark Horse and Comico) and Joe Nozemack were on hand to pass out the excellent Frank Miller and Simon Bisley magazine sized comic.

Both Pander Bros. were on hand, along with the ever lovely, eclectic artist Marne Lucas, and looked forward to Oni's January release of *Oni Double Feature,* an anthology featuring two 15 page stories in every issue. Issue #1 will serve the Pander Bros. Secret Broadcast and Matt Wagner illustrating Dir. Kevin Smith's (Clerks, Chasing Amy) tale of wayward heroes, Jay and Silent Bob in their first adventure. Driving up from Eugene, Oregon, was Suspense novelist Greg Rucka (Keeper, Finder) and wife Jen to talk art with Grendel Tales artist Steve Lieber on their upcoming four issue mini-series Whiteout. *Rust City* contributor, and creator of *Slave Labor's Caffeine,* Jim Hill was on hand, with no coffee in sight, as was Dark Horse editor Jamie Rich, complete with rubber shirt. Eisner award winning, beer brewing colorist Matt Hollinsworth emerged from underneath his deadline boulder to buy a few rounds but soon he and Mssr. Warnock stumbled away, not to be heard from again for the rest of the evening.

As much fun as the festivities were, the comics from Oni look to be even more fun. Their motto of "It's all about comics" says it all. They bring a love for the medium with them, excellent, diverse taste, and stay away from false hypes, gimmicks and crossovers all while working with people like Frank Miller, Kevin Smith, the Pander Bros., Troy Nixey, Paul Pope, Matt Wagner, Simon Bisley, Evan Dorkin, Shannon Wheeler and more. With so many comic companies out there floundering and pandering, it looks like a new bar has opened up that serves great drinks at reasonable prices. I especially can't wait for some of Kevin Smith's *View Askew* comics like Clerks to be served up. (6336 SE Milwaukie Ave., Suite #30, Portland, OR 97202. http://members.aol.com/onipress/index.html)

So, until next time, the bar is closed... now get your ass out of here.
C.K. Lichenstein II, ck2@teleport.com.

Matt Madden has been drawing comics for awhile now, and is starting to get a wee bit of notice.. finally! His ambitious mini-comic series *Terrifying Steamboat Stories* was one of the early impetus' to launch the anthology Top Shelf. In addition to T.S.S. Matt created a wonderfully disturbing 24-Hour mini *First Warning* , appeared in the now out-o-print Top Shelf #4, and has/will have, as his first major work nothing less a truly dark epic on the stands called *Black Candy* published by Black Eye. Gorgeous stuff. Matt & pal Jessica Able now reside in Mexico City .

Craig Thompson, who recently relocated to Portland OR from Milwaukee WI, is gonna be the next big thing in alternative comics. Seriously. He hit the scene with his stream-of-conscious mini-comic *My Friend Joey's Legs*, a diamond in the rough. His story here is his first foray into the larger comics realm. Watch for his solo opus *Good Bye, Chunky Rice*, coming soon from TSP. Craig, and his delightful roomy, cartoonist Kalah Allen, are also in transit, no permanent address as yet.

Rick Pinchera, Portland's secret weapon for the last several years, has recently moved on with his super coolio girlfriend Nancy to the East Coast. His book *CRUST* is a hoot, and can be ordered from TSP. 40 Sycamore St. #2, Providence RI 02909. (Rick and Nancy, we miss you, man!!)

Dean Haspiel is the prodigal New Yorker, fucking loco, balls 'o fire, drinking india ink for breakfast, with a Jim Beam chaser kind of guy... and a brother. Revelationary visions were had standing on the roof of his brownstone apartment, watching the sun set over Manhattan. (And i ain't talkin' about the exhibitionists living across the street!) He writes and draws the huggable adventures of *Billy Dogma*, and beginning with #5 will be publishing, with co-hort Josh Neufeld, their series *Keyhole* through TSP. 335 Court St., Suite 131, Brooklyn NY 11231

Brad Engle, only somewhat against his will, wears the fascist boots of a designer at the lovable Nike Empire. If you know of a job for him that could utilize his formidable design skills and pay a decent wage, contact us at our home office in Marietta, GA. He'd rather be snowboarding right now!

Hobo Mojo, simply continues to deliver the goods in exemplary fashion. For more info about *Fairvale* write to: Hobo Mojo Studio, Po Box 81192, Pittsburgh, PA 15217.

Marc Bell, the drifter, the grifter, the couch crasher.. Damn, what chops!!! He is currently shopping his series *Mojo Action Companion Unit* to publishers. Readers beware!! *M.A.C.U.* is one bent comic not intended for puny brains. I'll bet if you're nice you can get comics from Marc more fun than a Cherry Slurpee, and for about the same price. (Except that these comics will rot your brain, instead of your teeth.) 1016 Dalhousie Dr., London ONT N6K 1M7 Canada.

The beautiful **Gabby Gamboa** has returned to the pages of Top Shelf. Yes! (She appeared in TS2 with one of her all time best.) She still yields awesome power as one of the buyers at Last Gasp Comics/Distribution. Gabby is currently occupied with a work-in-progress graphic novel, which i for one can't wait to see. Po Box 170275, San Francisco CA 94117.

Dean Westerfield produces an assortment of funky-cool one-shot comics from sunny California, including *Take Care, Isis, Fishin'*, and with Jeff Guarino the excellent and appropriately titled flip-book *Flip*. The story contained herein is a prologue of sorts for a longer narrative. Something to keep a watch for, no? Po Box 20291, Fountain Valley, CA. 92728.

Alicia Rose, a.k.a. **Miss Murgatroid**, the Mistress of the Accordion, imbued the Top Shelf #5 Launch Party last September with her eerie musical sounds, and works for N.A.I.L. Distribution. (The story in this issue is reprinted from Bwana Spoons' seminal modern punk 'zine *Ain't Nothin' Like Fuckin' Moonshine*.) **Christine Shields** writes and draws *Blue Hole*, a haunting book if ever there was one. Her line is luscious and her paintings are to die for, honey. (Christine- if you read this, would you be interested in painting a cover for a future Top Shelf? Please, please, please, please, please..)

Brian Ralph, one of four strapping young lads residing at Fort Thunder in Providence, RI, draws the mighty *Fireball*. He also screenprints many/most of his own covers, and assorted projects, including a fabulous piece with David Sandlin for an event with The Million Year Picnic in Cambridge, Mass. His piece in the Highwater Books' anthology *Coober Skeeber*- featuring *The Man Thing, Silver Surfer, and Galactus*- kicks colossal fucking ass!! Po Box 2328, Providence RI 02906.

Warren Craghead, who happens to be this issues featured Xeric Grant Recipient, lived in Austin TX for a spell, moved to St. Louis MO for bit, and most recently planted his roots in New York NY, baby! His Xeric produced *Speedy* is truly a wonder to behold. Warren also makes some of the most delicious little handmade comics snacks that have to be seen to be believed. I have no idea how you could bribe him to get on his mailing list, but you can reach him at: Po Box 1285, Grand Central Station, New York NY 10163-1285.

James Kochalka Superstar really does get nekkid on stage!! It's true, i was there at the SPX '97 Opening Night Bash. James has a buttload of projects coming out this year, including stuff with Black Eye, Alternative Press, (maybe) Highwater Books, and from TSP, a Mini-Comics Compendium featuring his best from James Kochalka Superstar in the late Summer/early Fall. He's still got lots of comics available as well as his goofy rock & roll c.d./s at: Po Box 8321, Burlington VT 05402.

Ian Lynam & Simon Gane. Ian lives in San Francisco and Simon lives in England. Ian is part of the Migraine Comics Movement , while Simon looks to be one of the most prolific cartoonists around, making his own comics as well as working with Gavin Burrows, Peter Pavement, and Matt & Dave from *Scenes from the Inside*. Contact through TSP.

Jenny Zervakis makes the dreamy comic *Strange Growths*, a legend in the mini-comics subterranea. Along with her husband Mark Cunningham (another grizzled comics vet and fellow bartender) the two publish *Zoomcranks*, who's history is rich with ink-studs like Jennifer Daydreamer, David Lasky, Joe Chips, Scott Gilbert, John P., Jeff Zenick, Jake Austin, Jason Heller, Jerome Gaynor, JK Superstar, and Brian Ralph to name but a few. Jenny and Mark also qualify as some of the coolest/nicest folk in comics. 909 Lancaster, Durham NC 27701.

Pete Sickman-Garner. Ahhhh, Pete. What happened to you my friend, that has given you such a warped, sick sense of humor. I fail to believe that it's the sole fault of working at a retail bookstore. At any rate, Pete produces comics so god damned funny it's frightening. (In league with our master of laughter Sam Hendersen.) Coming soon from TSP is the Mini-Comics Compendium of Pete's *Hey, Mister* minis, with his regular solo book resuming just mere months later, published by TSP as well. 1530 Cedar St., Fayetteville AR 53703.

Jeff Zenick. lives mere blocks from where i used to live in Eugene, but i for the life of me couldn't find his digs the last two times i was down. Nonetheless, Jeff has produced an impressive travelog in illustrated journal form, that is quite a pleasurable read. Look for his books in John P.'s *Spit and a Half* catalog, or write to Jeff himself for more info at: Po Box 877 Tallahassee FL 32302.

Steven (Ribs!) Weissman draws comics for Marvel.. what a miserable, spineless sellout! (Marvel Visions fan mag--by bejeezus it's awful fun stuff!) He is also now being published by juggernaut publisher Jeff Mason and his Alternative Press. *Tikes! and Yikes!* are arguably some of the niftiest comics around. If you haven't seen 'em, well.. get with the program, doofus. 564 Market St. Suite 720, San Francisco CA 94133.

Alan Hunt self-publishes a wonderful, if not a little disturbing,mini-comic titled *Out There*. His comic was an Ignatz Nominee for "Best Mini" at SPX '97, and comes highly recommended. Alan can be reached at: 116 Garnet Ave., Toronto ONT M6G 1V7.

COMRADES SIX

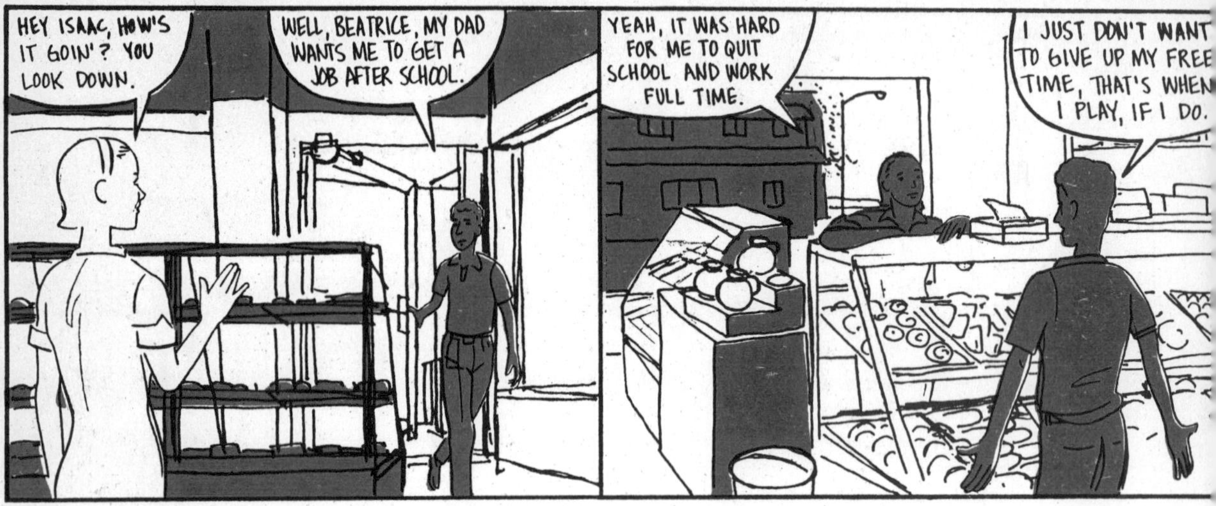
HEY ISAAC, HOW'S IT GOIN'? YOU LOOK DOWN.
WELL, BEATRICE, MY DAD WANTS ME TO GET A JOB AFTER SCHOOL.
YEAH, IT WAS HARD FOR ME TO QUIT SCHOOL AND WORK FULL TIME.
I JUST DON'T WANT TO GIVE UP MY FREE TIME, THAT'S WHEN I PLAY, IF I DO.

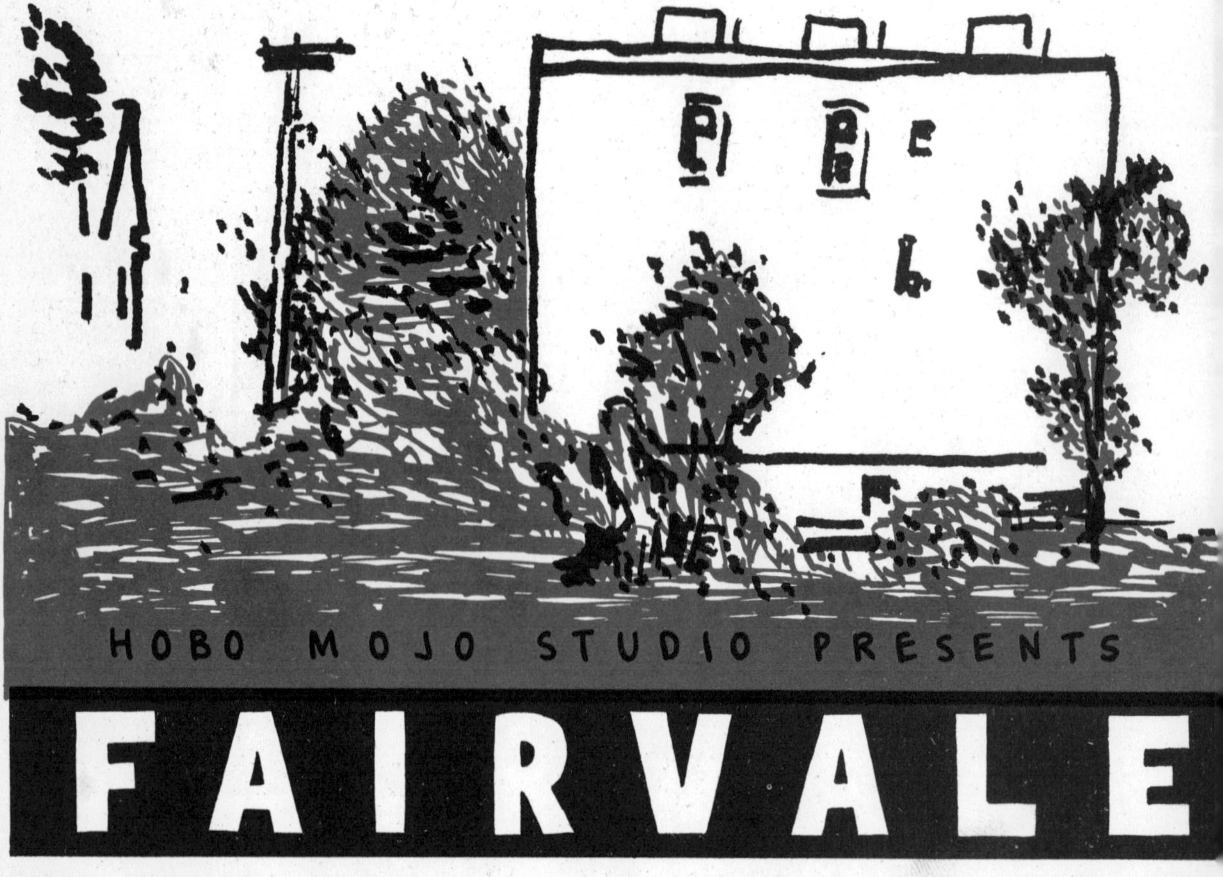
HOBO MOJO STUDIO PRESENTS
FAIRVALE

ISAAC'S FATHER WANTS HIS SON TO ABANDON HIS MUSICAL AMBITIONS. "HOW ARE YOU EVER GOING TO MAKE A LIVING?"

NO I JUST SIT HERE. I CAN'T EVEN PLAY A NOTE. I KEEP THINKING OF WHEN I HAFTA GO LOOK FOR A JOB.

I USED TO PLAY ALL DAY. I WAS GOOD. BUT NOW, I DUNNO, I'M ALL CONFUSED.

WHEN I SIT DOWN TO PLAY, I GET SCARED. I START TO WONDER IF I'M GOOD ENOUGH. I NEVER USED TO THINK THAT WAY.

I MEAN, NOW, I'M CONCERNED WITH PLAYING FOR MONEY, COULD I EVEN GET A GIG SOMEWHERE? AND EVEN IF I DID, WOULD MY DAD CONSIDER IT A JOB?

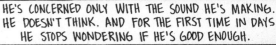

I DON'T KNOW, ISAAC...

...IT'LL WORK OUT.

HE'S NOT SURPRISED WHEN HE SITS DOWN AND TOUCHES THE KEYS AGAIN. HE CAN'T BE SURE, THOUGH, WHAT PUSHED HIM TO SIT AND PLAY. HIS FATHER? BEATRICE?

HE'S CONCERNED ONLY WITH THE SOUND HE'S MAKING. HE DOESN'T THINK. AND FOR THE FIRST TIME IN DAYS HE STOPS WONDERING IF HE'S GOOD ENOUGH.

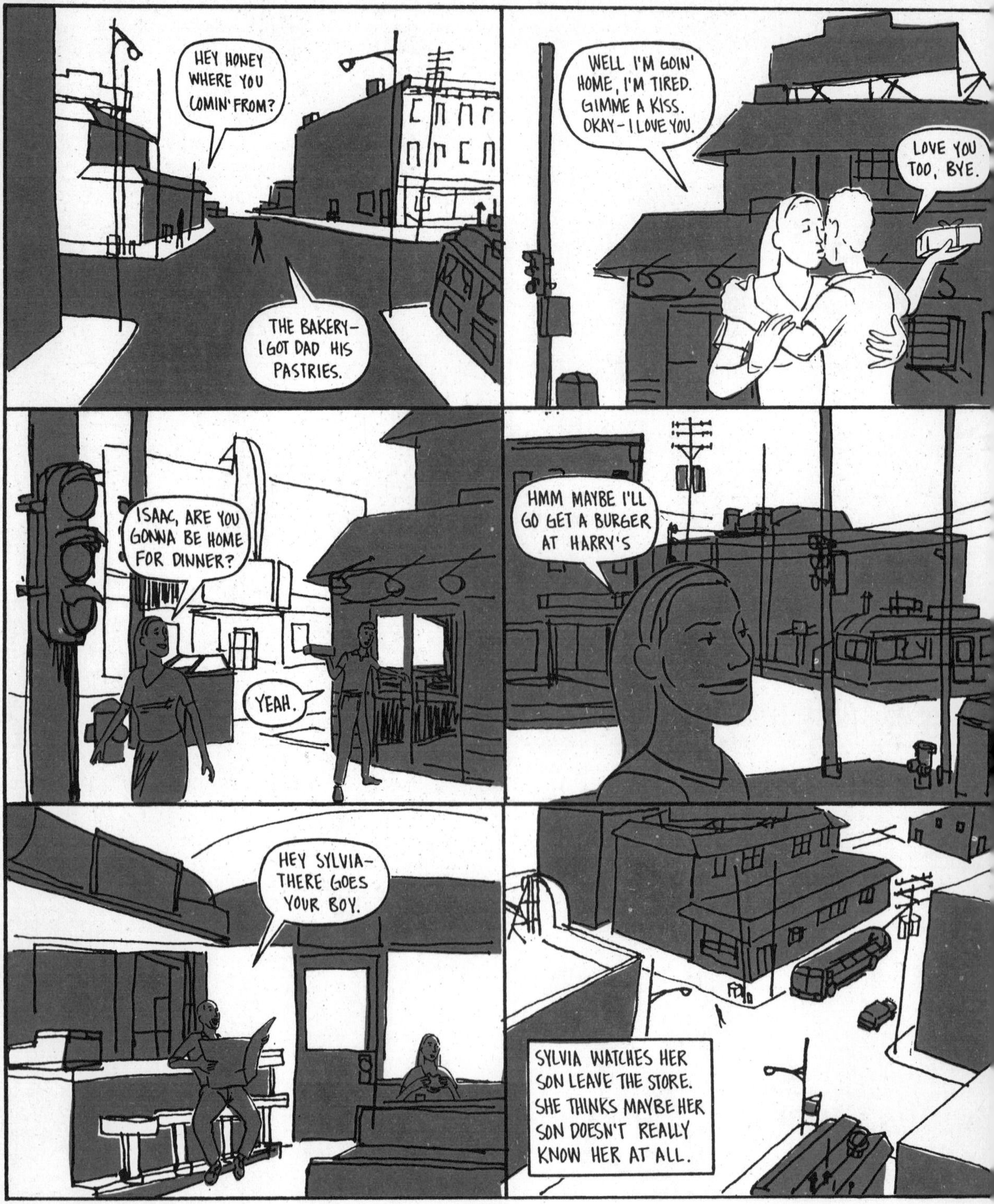
HEY HONEY WHERE YOU COMIN' FROM?
THE BAKERY- I GOT DAD HIS PASTRIES.
WELL I'M GOIN' HOME, I'M TIRED. GIMME A KISS. OKAY- I LOVE YOU.
LOVE YOU TOO, BYE.
ISAAC, ARE YOU GONNA BE HOME FOR DINNER?
YEAH.
HMM MAYBE I'LL GO GET A BURGER AT HARRY'S
HEY SYLVIA- THERE GOES YOUR BOY.
SYLVIA WATCHES HER SON LEAVE THE STORE. SHE THINKS MAYBE HER SON DOESN'T REALLY KNOW HER AT ALL.

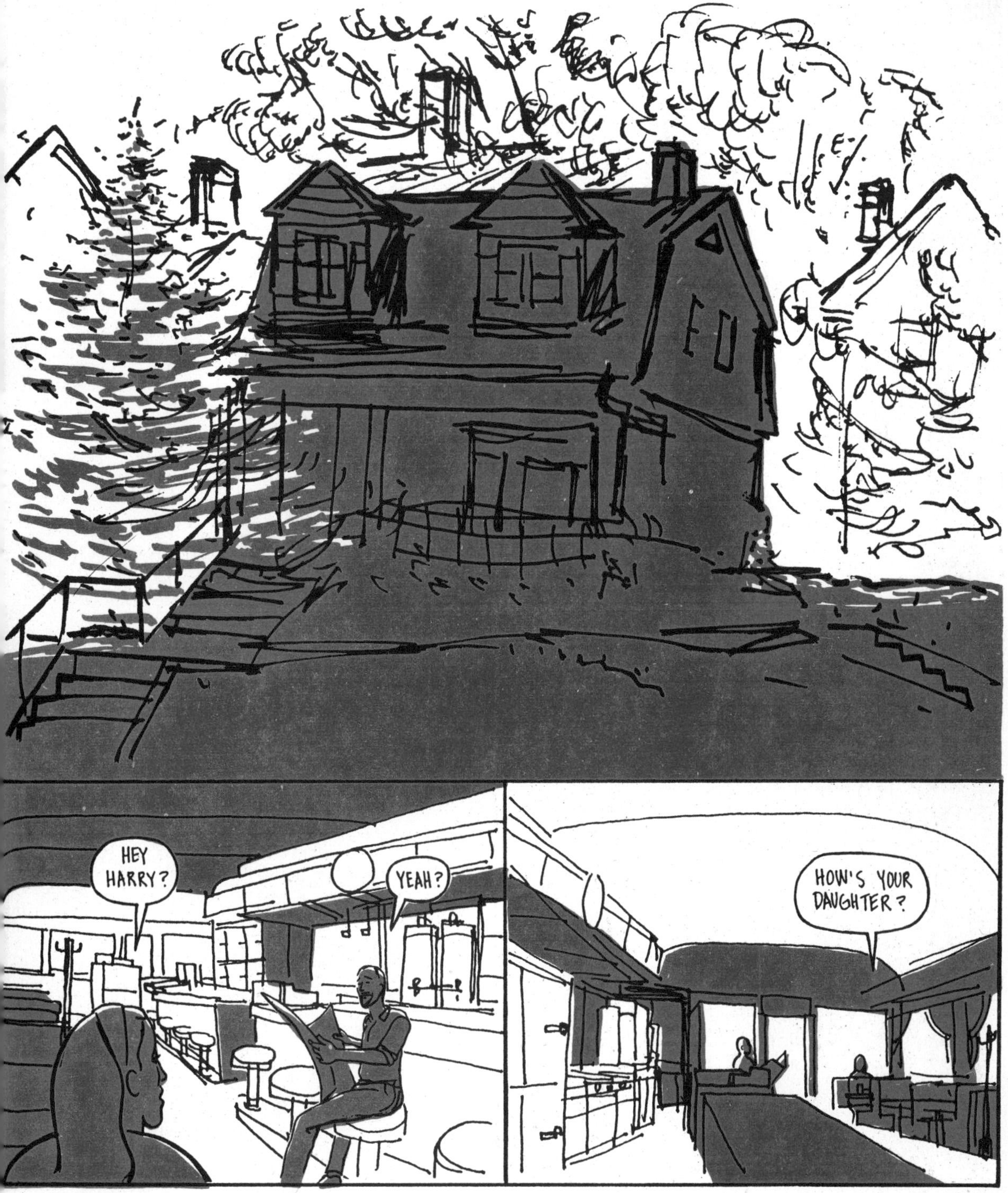

HEY HARRY?
YEAH?
HOW'S YOUR DAUGHTER?

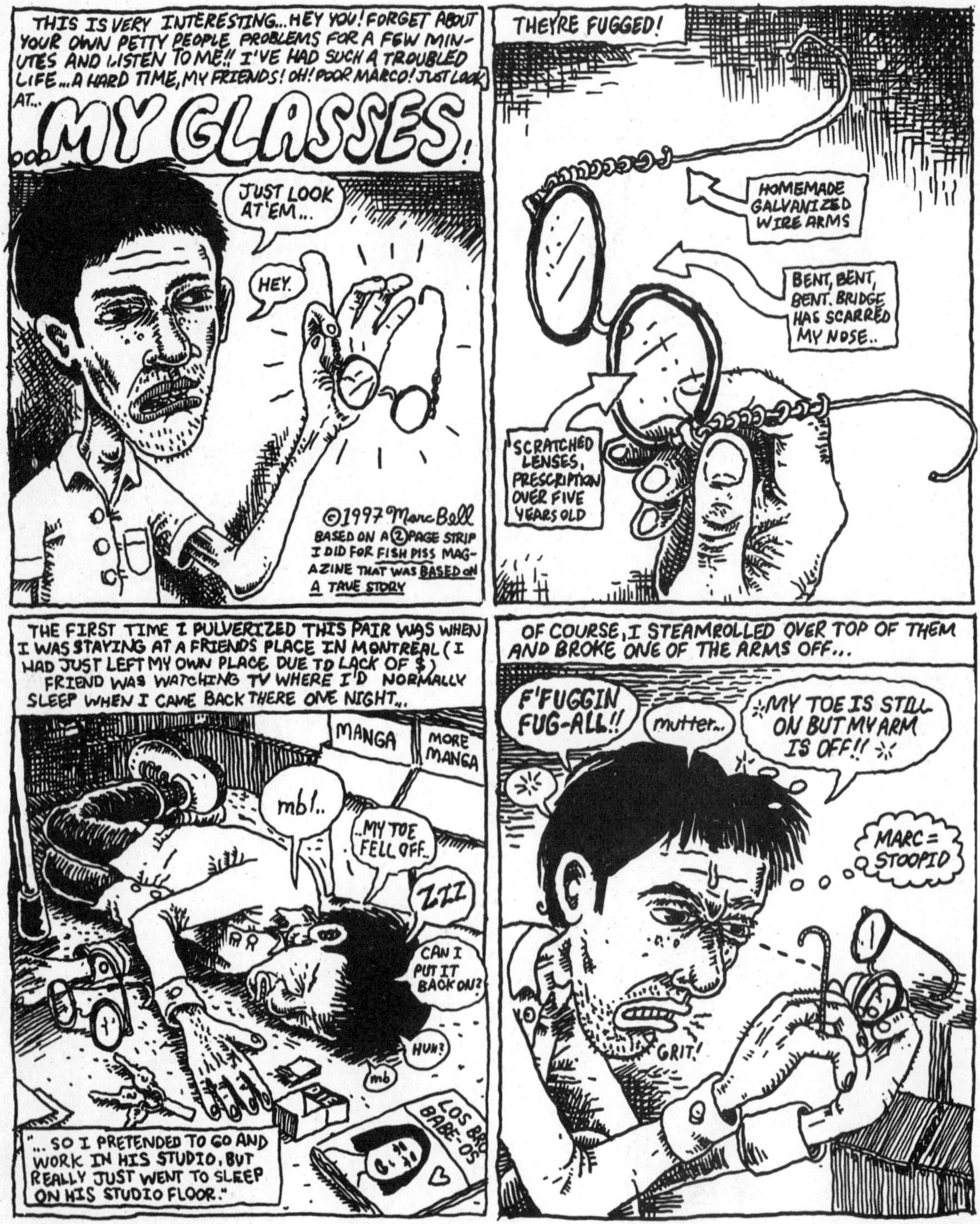
THIS IS VERY INTERESTING... HEY YOU! FORGET ABOUT YOUR OWN PETTY PEOPLE PROBLEMS FOR A FEW MINUTES AND LISTEN TO ME!! I'VE HAD SUCH A TROUBLED LIFE... A HARD TIME, MY FRIENDS! OH! POOR MARCO! JUST LOOK AT...
...MY GLASSES!
JUST LOOK AT'EM...
HEY.
©1997 Marc Bell
BASED ON A 2 PAGE STRIP I DID FOR FISH PISS MAGAZINE THAT WAS BASED ON A TRUE STORY
THEY'RE FUGGED!
HOMEMADE GALVANIZED WIRE ARMS
BENT, BENT, BENT. BRIDGE HAS SCARRED MY NOSE..
SCRATCHED LENSES, PRESCRIPTION OVER FIVE YEARS OLD
THE FIRST TIME I PULVERIZED THIS PAIR WAS WHEN I WAS STAYING AT A FRIENDS PLACE IN MONTREAL (I HAD JUST LEFT MY OWN PLACE DUE TO LACK OF $) FRIEND WAS WATCHING TV WHERE I'D NORMALLY SLEEP WHEN I CAME BACK THERE ONE NIGHT...
MANGA
MORE MANGA
mbl..
..MY TOE FELL OFF..
ZZZ
CAN I PUT IT BACK ON?
HUH?
mb
LOS BRO BABE-OS
"...SO I PRETENDED TO GO AND WORK IN HIS STUDIO, BUT REALLY JUST WENT TO SLEEP ON HIS STUDIO FLOOR."
OF COURSE, I STEAMROLLED OVER TOP OF THEM AND BROKE ONE OF THE ARMS OFF...
F'FUGGIN FUG-ALL!!
mutter..
MY TOE IS STILL ON BUT MY ARM IS OFF!!
MARC = STOOPID
GRIT!

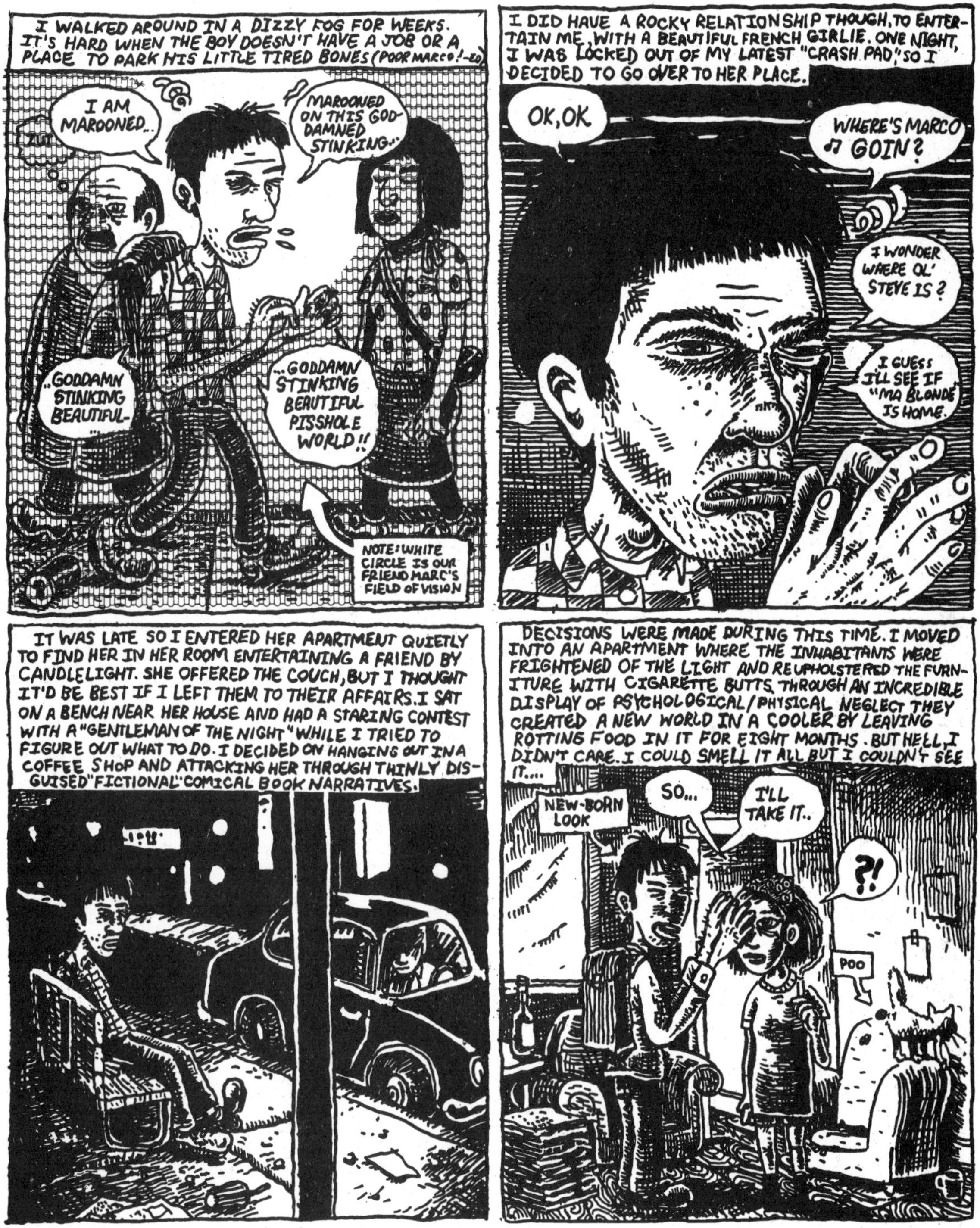

I WALKED AROUND IN A DIZZY FOG FOR WEEKS. IT'S HARD WHEN THE BOY DOESN'T HAVE A JOB OR A PLACE TO PARK HIS LITTLE TIRED BONES (POOR MARCO! -ED)
ZUT
I AM MAROONED..
MAROONED ON THIS GOD-DAMNED STINKING..
..GODDAMN STINKING BEAUTIFUL-...
...GODDAMN STINKING BEAUTIFUL PISSHOLE WORLD!!
NOTE: WHITE CIRCLE IS OUR FRIEND MARC'S FIELD OF VISION
I DID HAVE A ROCKY RELATIONSHIP THOUGH, TO ENTERTAIN ME, WITH A BEAUTIFUL FRENCH GIRLIE. ONE NIGHT, I WAS LOCKED OUT OF MY LATEST "CRASH PAD," SO I DECIDED TO GO OVER TO HER PLACE.
OK, OK
WHERE'S MARCO ♫ GOIN?
I WONDER WHERE OL' STEVE IS?
I GUESS I'LL SEE IF "MA BLONDE" IS HOME.
IT WAS LATE SO I ENTERED HER APARTMENT QUIETLY TO FIND HER IN HER ROOM ENTERTAINING A FRIEND BY CANDLELIGHT. SHE OFFERED THE COUCH, BUT I THOUGHT IT'D BE BEST IF I LEFT THEM TO THEIR AFFAIRS. I SAT ON A BENCH NEAR HER HOUSE AND HAD A STARING CONTEST WITH A "GENTLEMAN OF THE NIGHT" WHILE I TRIED TO FIGURE OUT WHAT TO DO. I DECIDED ON HANGING OUT IN A COFFEE SHOP AND ATTACKING HER THROUGH THINLY DISGUISED "FICTIONAL" COMICAL BOOK NARRATIVES.
DECISIONS WERE MADE DURING THIS TIME. I MOVED INTO AN APARTMENT WHERE THE INHABITANTS WERE FRIGHTENED OF THE LIGHT AND REUPHOLSTERED THE FURNITURE WITH CIGARETTE BUTTS. THROUGH AN INCREDIBLE DISPLAY OF PSYCHOLOGICAL/PHYSICAL NEGLECT THEY CREATED A NEW WORLD IN A COOLER BY LEAVING ROTTING FOOD IN IT FOR EIGHT MONTHS. BUT HELL, I DIDN'T CARE. I COULD SMELL IT ALL BUT I COULDN'T SEE IT....
NEW-BORN LOOK
SO...
I'LL TAKE IT..
?!
POO

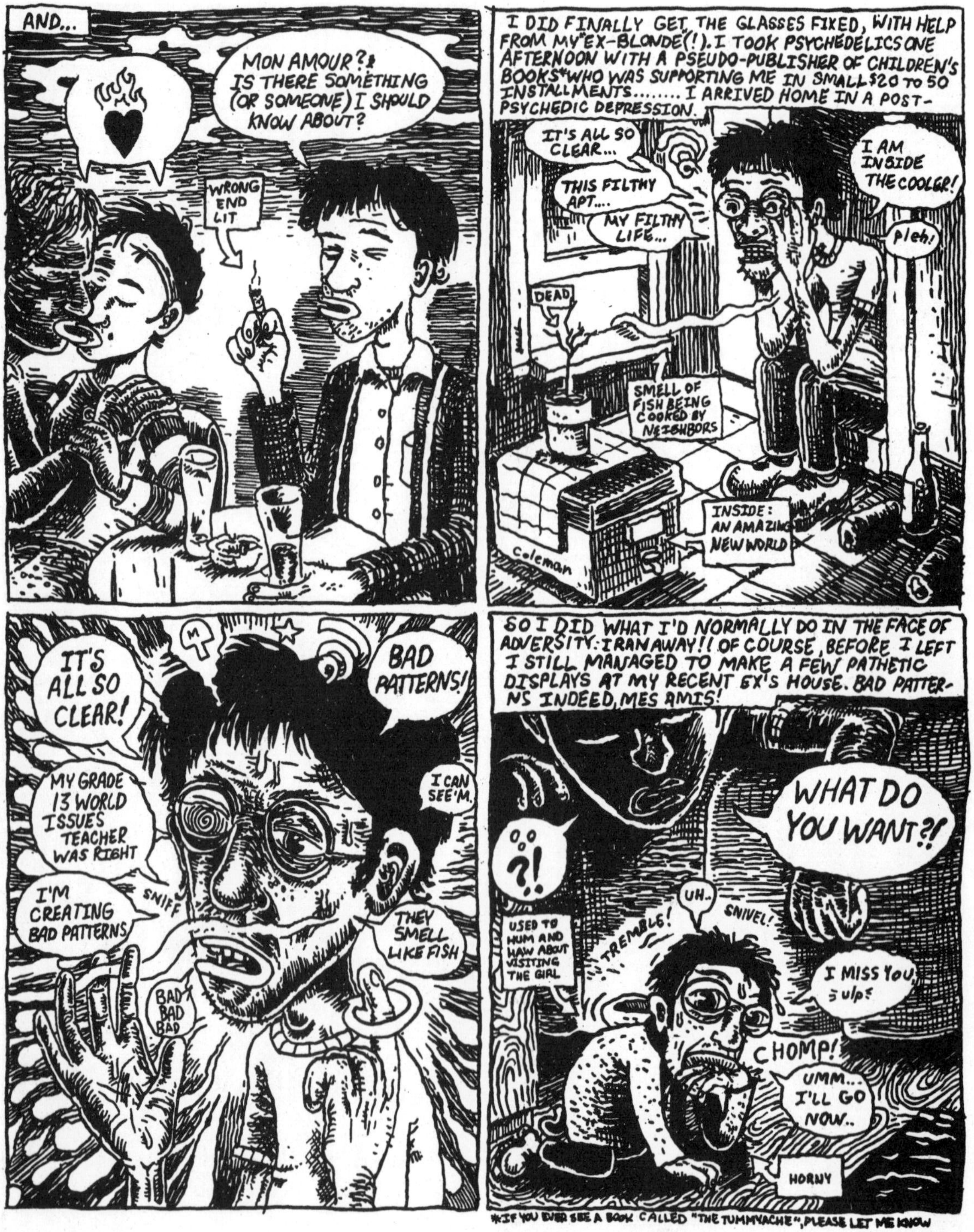
AND...
MON AMOUR?! IS THERE SOMETHING (OR SOMEONE) I SHOULD KNOW ABOUT?
WRONG END LIT
I DID FINALLY GET THE GLASSES FIXED, WITH HELP FROM MY "EX-BLONDE"(!). I TOOK PSYCHEDELICS ONE AFTERNOON WITH A PSEUDO-PUBLISHER OF CHILDREN'S BOOKS* WHO WAS SUPPORTING ME IN SMALL $20 TO 50 INSTALLMENTS........ I ARRIVED HOME IN A POST-PSYCHEDIC DEPRESSION.
IT'S ALL SO CLEAR...
THIS FILTHY APT....
MY FILTHY LIFE...
I AM INSIDE THE COOLER!
pleh!
DEAD
SMELL OF FISH BEING COOKED BY NEIGHBORS
INSIDE: AN AMAZING NEW WORLD
Coleman
IT'S ALL SO CLEAR!
BAD PATTERNS!
MY GRADE 13 WORLD ISSUES TEACHER WAS RIGHT
I CAN SEE'M.
I'M CREATING BAD PATTERNS
SNIFF
THEY SMELL LIKE FISH
BAD BAD BAD
SO I DID WHAT I'D NORMALLY DO IN THE FACE OF ADVERSITY: I RAN AWAY!! OF COURSE, BEFORE I LEFT I STILL MANAGED TO MAKE A FEW PATHETIC DISPLAYS AT MY RECENT EX'S HOUSE. BAD PATTERNS INDEED, MES AMIS!
WHAT DO YOU WANT?!
?!
UH..
SNIVEL!
TREMBLE!
USED TO HUM AND HAW ABOUT VISITING THE GIRL
I MISS YOU
ulp
CHOMP!
UMM... I'LL GO NOW..
HORNY

*IF YOU EVER SEE A BOOK CALLED "THE TUMMYACHE", PLEASE LET ME KNOW

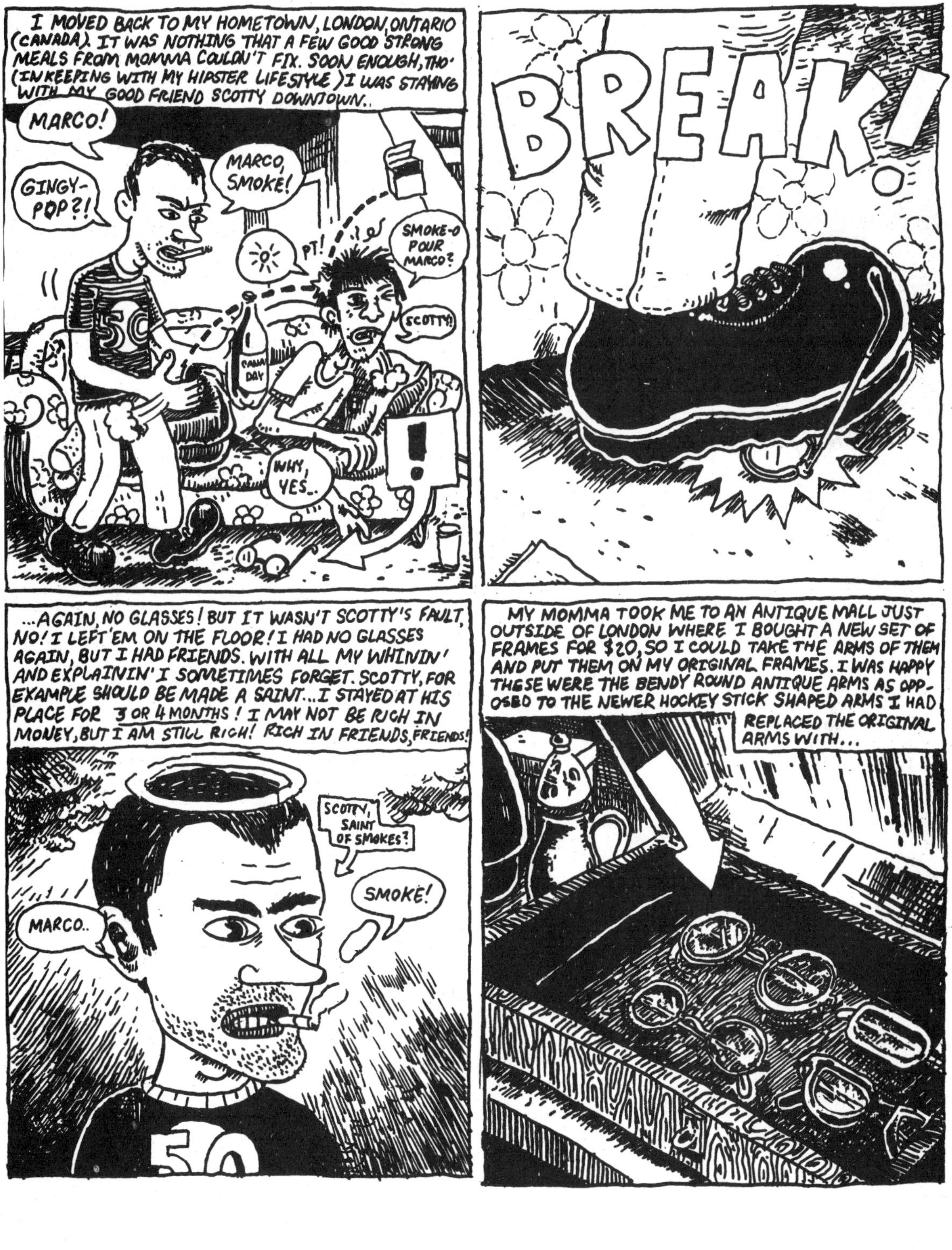
I MOVED BACK TO MY HOMETOWN, LONDON, ONTARIO (CANADA). IT WAS NOTHING THAT A FEW GOOD STRONG MEALS FROM MOMMA COULDN'T FIX. SOON ENOUGH, THO' (IN KEEPING WITH MY HIPSTER LIFESTYLE) I WAS STAYING WITH MY GOOD FRIEND SCOTTY DOWNTOWN..
MARCO!
GINGY-POP?!
MARCO, SMOKE!
PT!
SMOKE-O POUR MARCO?
SCOTTY!
WHY, YES..
!
BREAK!
...AGAIN, NO GLASSES! BUT IT WASN'T SCOTTY'S FAULT, NO! I LEFT 'EM ON THE FLOOR! I HAD NO GLASSES AGAIN, BUT I HAD FRIENDS. WITH ALL MY WHININ' AND EXPLAININ' I SOMETIMES FORGET. SCOTTY, FOR EXAMPLE SHOULD BE MADE A SAINT... I STAYED AT HIS PLACE FOR 3 OR 4 MONTHS! I MAY NOT BE RICH IN MONEY, BUT I AM STILL RICH! RICH IN FRIENDS, FRIENDS!
SCOTTY, SAINT OF SMOKES?
SMOKE!
MARCO..
MY MOMMA TOOK ME TO AN ANTIQUE MALL JUST OUTSIDE OF LONDON WHERE I BOUGHT A NEW SET OF FRAMES FOR $20, SO I COULD TAKE THE ARMS OF THEM AND PUT THEM ON MY ORIGINAL FRAMES. I WAS HAPPY THESE WERE THE BENDY ROUND ANTIQUE ARMS AS OPPOSED TO THE NEWER HOCKEY STICK SHAPED ARMS I HAD REPLACED THE ORIGINAL ARMS WITH...

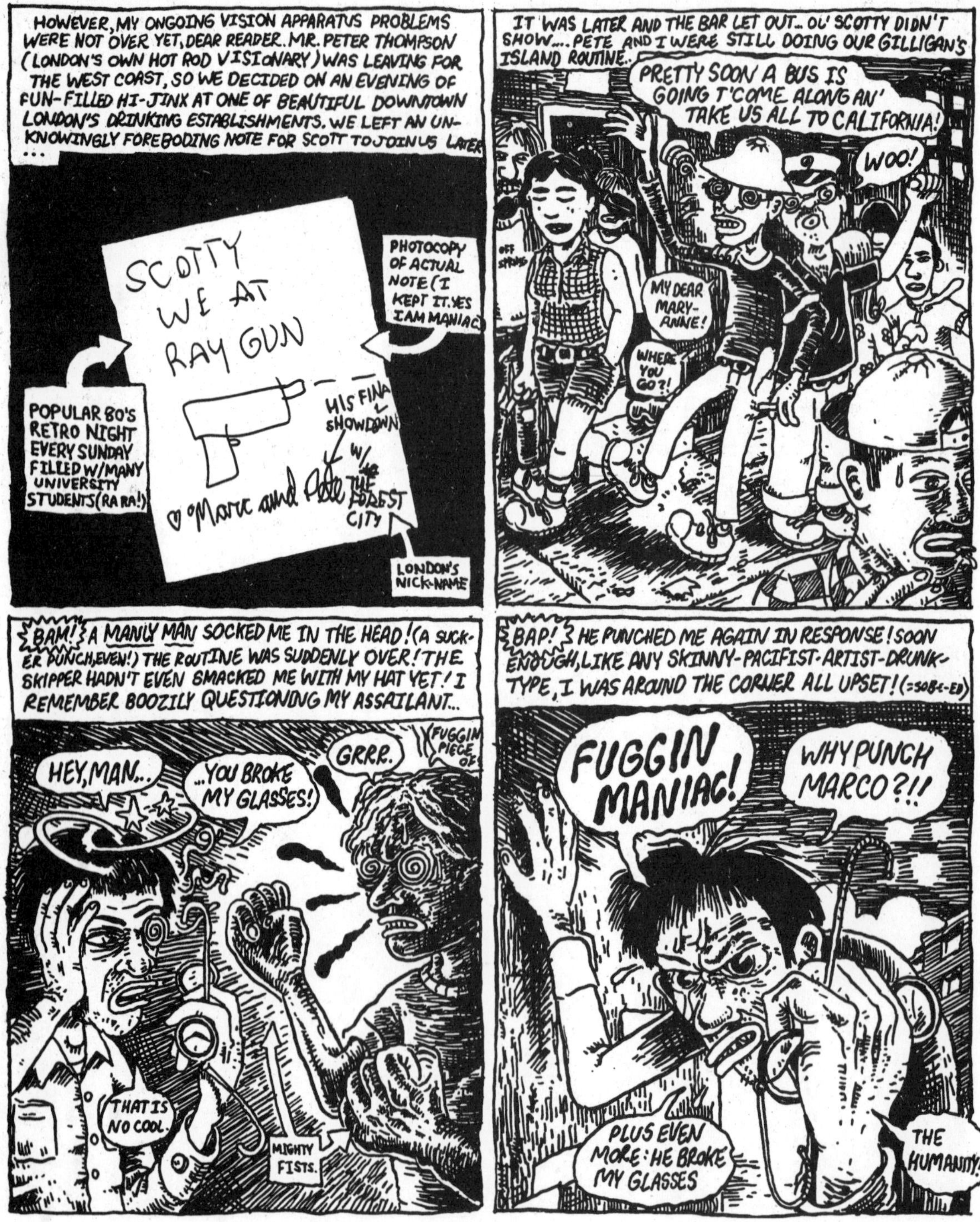
HOWEVER, MY ONGOING VISION APPARATUS PROBLEMS WERE NOT OVER YET, DEAR READER.. MR. PETER THOMPSON (LONDON'S OWN HOT ROD VISIONARY) WAS LEAVING FOR THE WEST COAST, SO WE DECIDED ON AN EVENING OF FUN-FILLED HI-JINX AT ONE OF BEAUTIFUL DOWNTOWN LONDON'S DRINKING ESTABLISHMENTS. WE LEFT AN UNKNOWINGLY FOREBODING NOTE FOR SCOTT TO JOIN US LATER...
SCOTTY WE AT RAY GUN
HIS FINAL SHOWDOWN W/ THE FOREST CITY
♡ Marc and Pete
PHOTOCOPY OF ACTUAL NOTE (I KEPT IT. YES I AM MANIAC)
POPULAR 80'S RETRO NIGHT EVERY SUNDAY FILLED W/MANY UNIVERSITY STUDENTS (RA RA!)
LONDON'S NICK-NAME
IT WAS LATER AND THE BAR LET OUT.. OL' SCOTTY DIDN'T SHOW.... PETE AND I WERE STILL DOING OUR GILLIGAN'S ISLAND ROUTINE..
PRETTY SOON A BUS IS GOING T'COME ALONG AN' TAKE US ALL TO CALIFORNIA!
WOO!
MY DEAR MARY-ANNE!
WHERE YOU GO?!
BAM! A MANLY MAN SOCKED ME IN THE HEAD! (A SUCKER PUNCH, EVEN!) THE ROUTINE WAS SUDDENLY OVER! THE SKIPPER HADN'T EVEN SMACKED ME WITH MY HAT YET! I REMEMBER BOOZILY QUESTIONING MY ASSAILANT...
HEY, MAN...
...YOU BROKE MY GLASSES!
GRRR.
FUGGIN PIECE OF
THAT IS NO COOL.
MIGHTY FISTS.
BAP! HE PUNCHED ME AGAIN IN RESPONSE! SOON ENOUGH, LIKE ANY SKINNY-PACIFIST-ARTIST-DRUNK-TYPE, I WAS AROUND THE CORNER ALL UPSET! (=SOB-E-ED)
FUGGIN MANIAC!
WHY PUNCH MARCO?!!
PLUS EVEN MORE: HE BROKE MY GLASSES
THE HUMANITY!

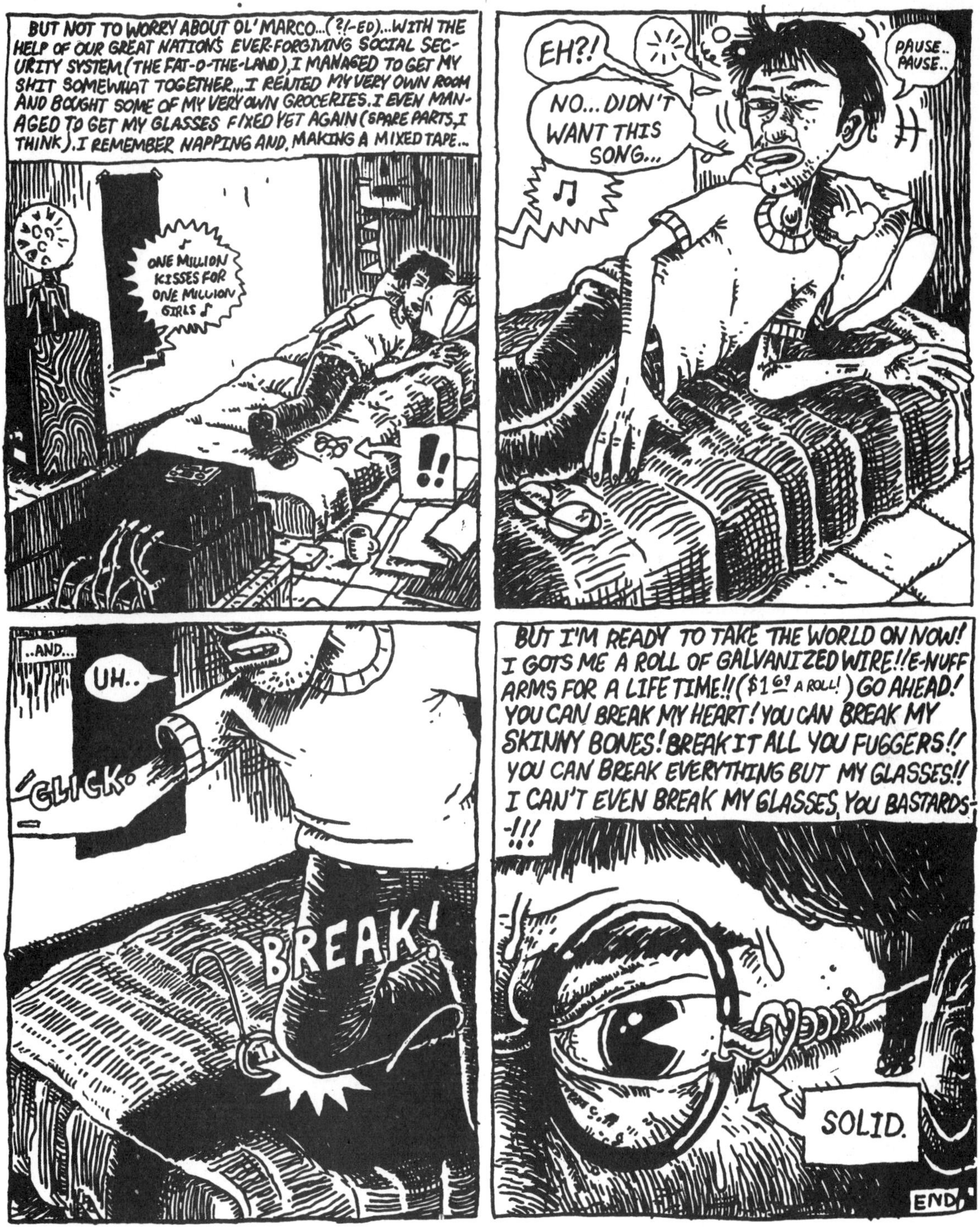
BUT NOT TO WORRY ABOUT OL' MARCO...(?!-ED)...WITH THE HELP OF OUR GREAT NATION'S EVER-FORGIVING SOCIAL SECURITY SYSTEM (THE FAT-O-THE-LAND), I MANAGED TO GET MY SHIT SOMEWHAT TOGETHER...I RENTED MY VERY OWN ROOM AND BOUGHT SOME OF MY VERY OWN GROCERIES. I EVEN MANAGED TO GET MY GLASSES FIXED YET AGAIN (SPARE PARTS, I THINK). I REMEMBER NAPPING AND MAKING A MIXED TAPE...
ONE MILLION KISSES FOR ONE MILLION GIRLS
!!
EH?!
NO... DIDN'T WANT THIS SONG...
PAUSE.. PAUSE..
..AND..
UH..
CLICK
BREAK!
BUT I'M READY TO TAKE THE WORLD ON NOW! I GOTS ME A ROLL OF GALVANIZED WIRE!! E-NUFF ARMS FOR A LIFE TIME!! ($1.69 A ROLL!) GO AHEAD! YOU CAN BREAK MY HEART! YOU CAN BREAK MY SKINNY BONES! BREAK IT ALL YOU FUGGERS!! YOU CAN BREAK EVERYTHING BUT MY GLASSES!! I CAN'T EVEN BREAK MY GLASSES, YOU BASTARDS-!!!
SOLID.
END

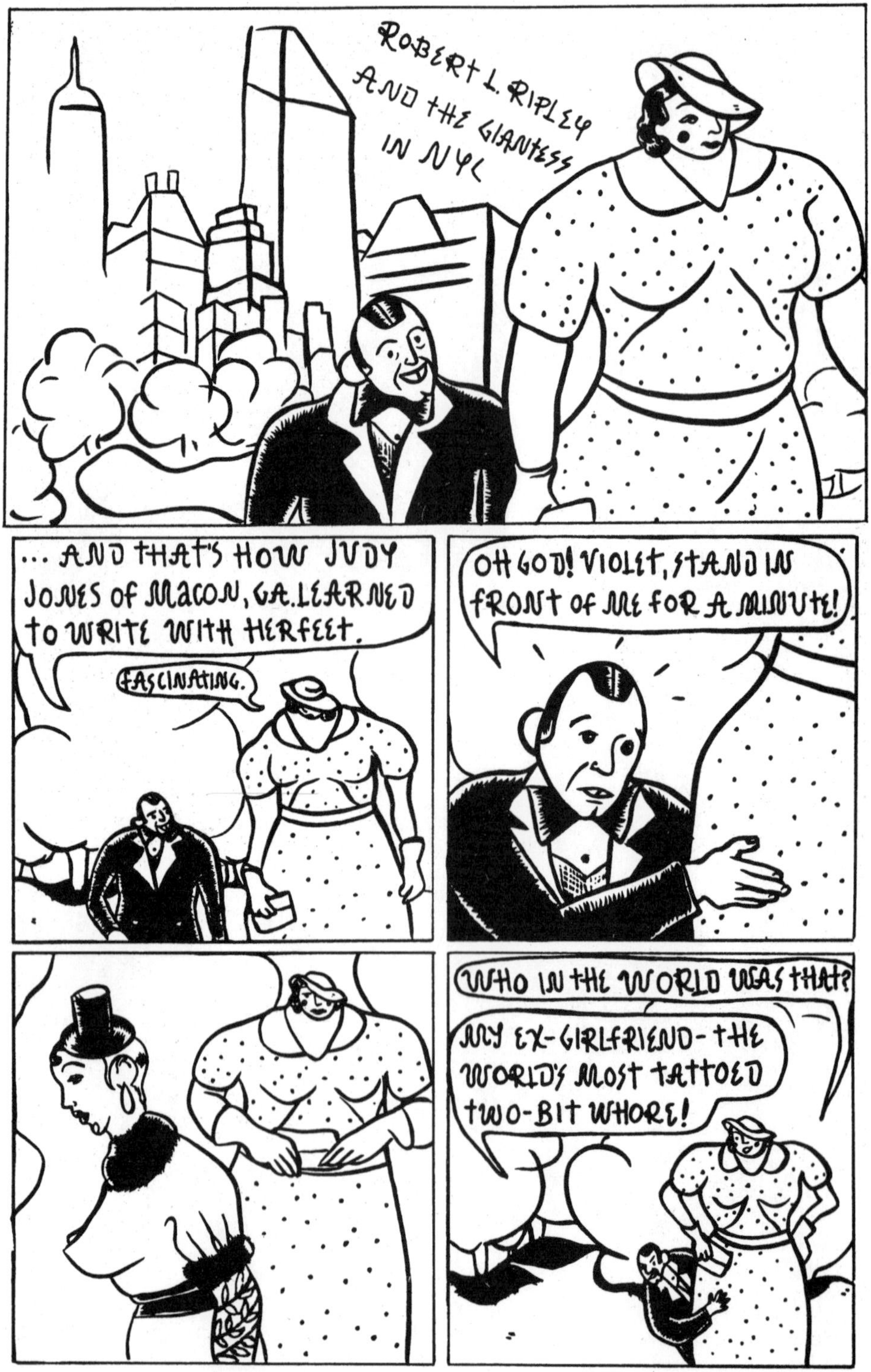
ROBERT L. RIPLEY AND THE GIANTESS IN NYC
... AND THAT'S HOW JUDY JONES OF MACON, GA. LEARNED TO WRITE WITH HER FEET.
FASCINATING.
OH GOD! VIOLET, STAND IN FRONT OF ME FOR A MINUTE!
WHO IN THE WORLD WAS THAT?
MY EX-GIRLFRIEND - THE WORLD'S MOST TATTOED TWO-BIT WHORE!

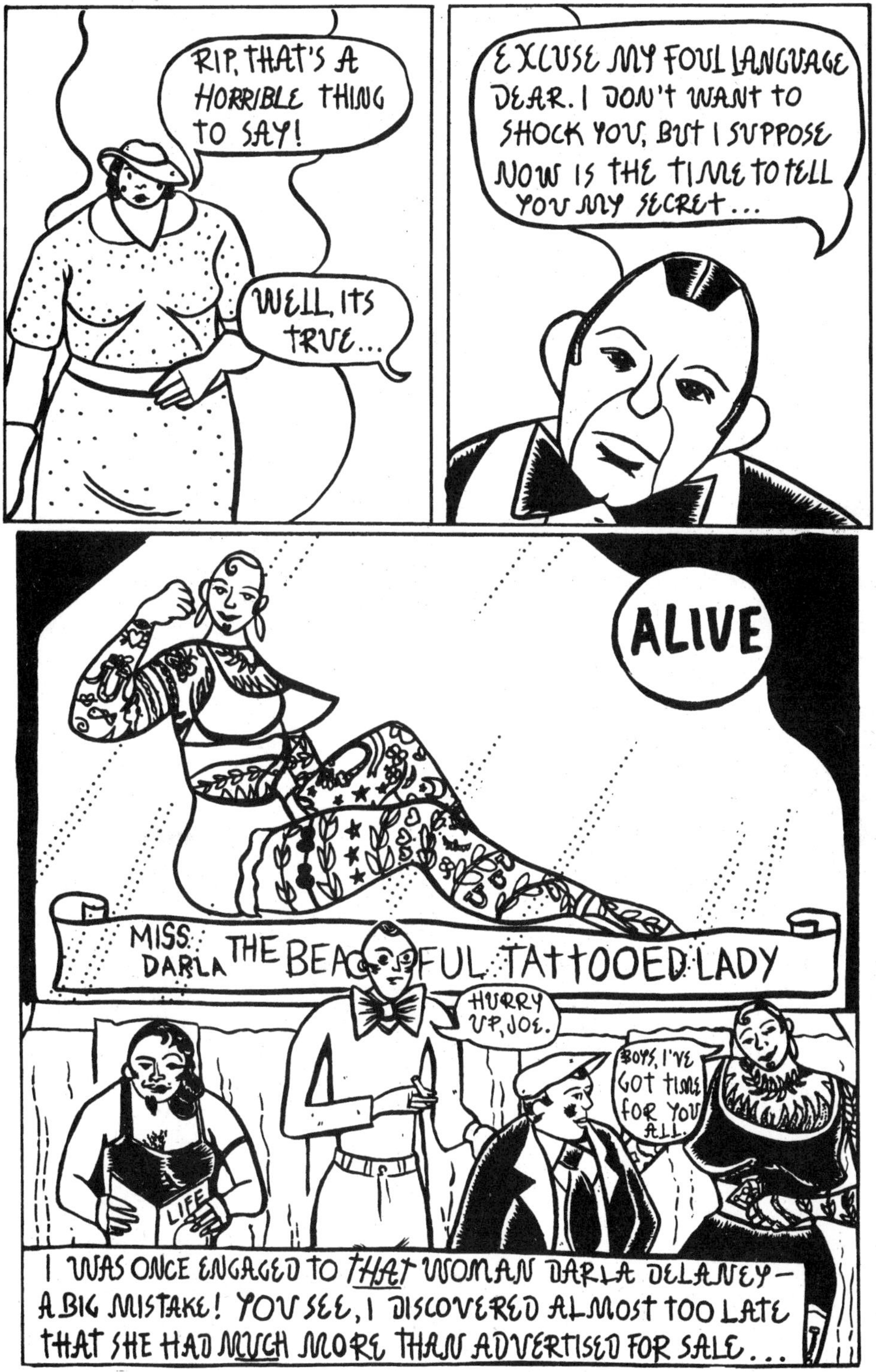
RIP, THAT'S A HORRIBLE THING TO SAY!
WELL, ITS TRUE...
EXCUSE MY FOUL LANGUAGE DEAR. I DON'T WANT TO SHOCK YOU, BUT I SUPPOSE NOW IS THE TIME TO TELL YOU MY SECRET...
ALIVE
MISS DARLA THE BEA FUL TATTOOED LADY
HURRY UP, JOE.
BOYS, I'VE GOT TIME FOR YOU ALL.
LIFE
I WAS ONCE ENGAGED TO THAT WOMAN DARLA DELANEY— A BIG MISTAKE! YOU SEE, I DISCOVERED ALMOST TOO LATE THAT SHE HAD MUCH MORE THAN ADVERTISED FOR SALE...

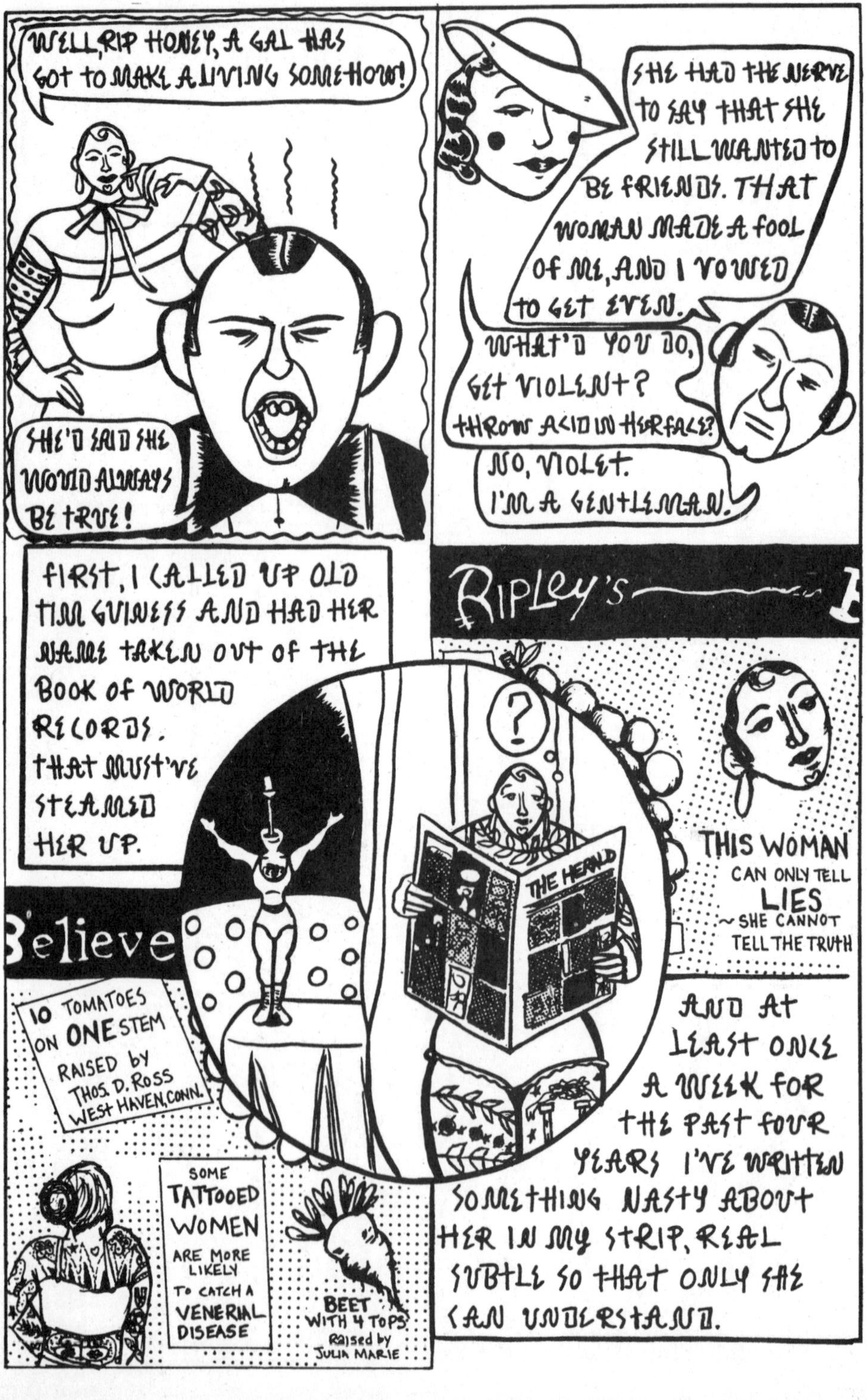
WELL, RIP HONEY, A GAL HAS GOT TO MAKE A LIVING SOMEHOW!
SHE'D SAID SHE WOULD ALWAYS BE TRUE!
SHE HAD THE NERVE TO SAY THAT SHE STILL WANTED TO BE FRIENDS. THAT WOMAN MADE A FOOL OF ME, AND I VOWED TO GET EVEN.
WHAT'D YOU DO, GET VIOLENT? THROW ACID IN HER FACE?
NO, VIOLET. I'M A GENTLEMAN.
FIRST, I CALLED UP OLD TIM GUINESS AND HAD HER NAME TAKEN OUT OF THE BOOK OF WORLD RECORDS. THAT MUST'VE STEAMED HER UP.
Ripley's
Believe
THE HERALD
THIS WOMAN CAN ONLY TELL LIES ~ SHE CANNOT TELL THE TRUTH
10 TOMATOES ON ONE STEM RAISED by THOS. D. ROSS WEST HAVEN, CONN.
SOME TATTOOED WOMEN ARE MORE LIKELY TO CATCH A VENERIAL DISEASE
BEET WITH 4 TOPS Raised by JULIA MARIE
AND AT LEAST ONCE A WEEK FOR THE PAST FOUR YEARS I'VE WRITTEN SOMETHING NASTY ABOUT HER IN MY STRIP, REAL SUBTLE SO THAT ONLY SHE CAN UNDERSTAND.

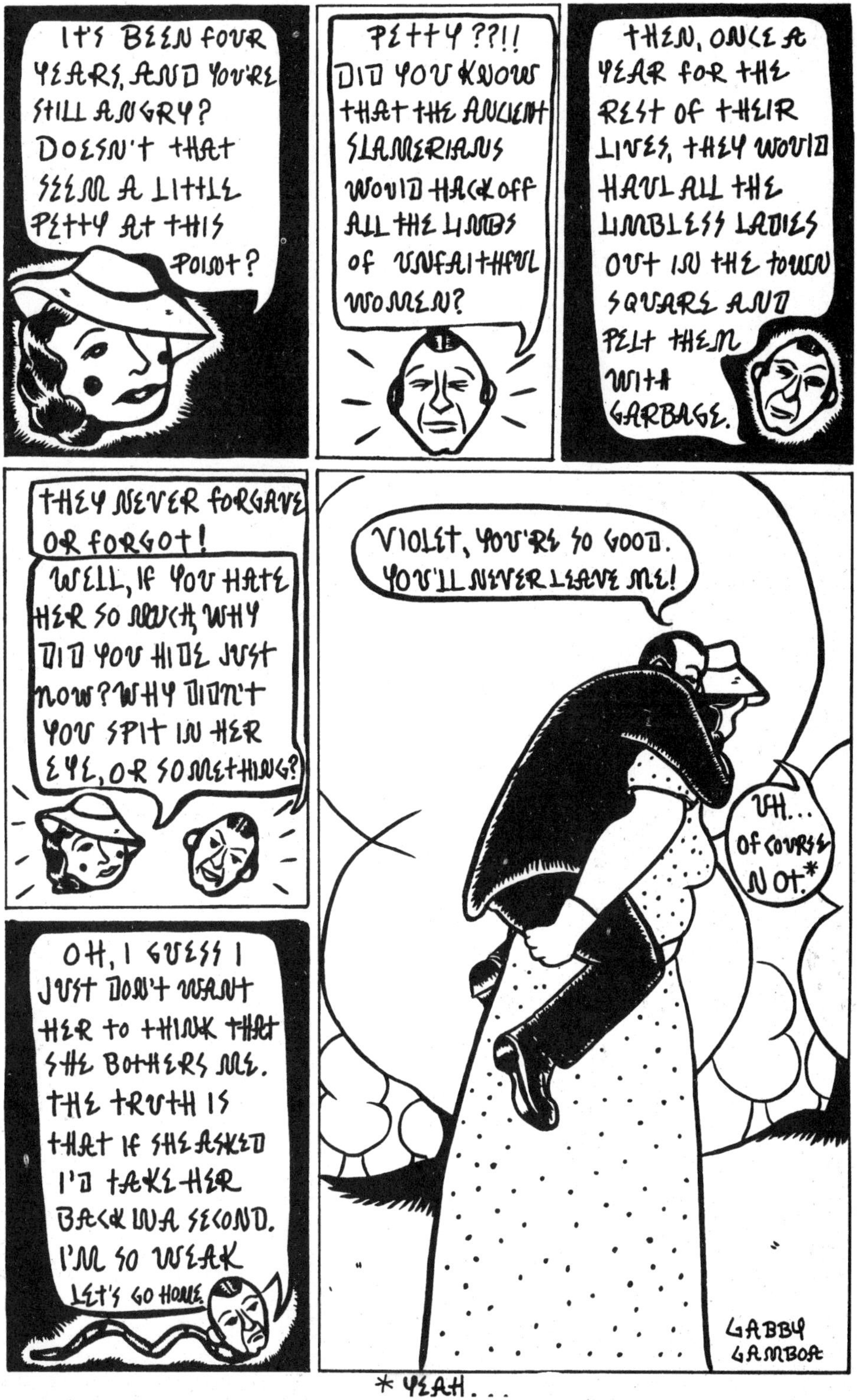

IT'S BEEN FOUR YEARS, AND YOU'RE STILL ANGRY? DOESN'T THAT SEEM A LITTLE PETTY AT THIS POINT?
PETTY??!! DID YOU KNOW THAT THE ANCIENT SLAMERIANS WOULD HACK OFF ALL THE LIMBS OF UNFAITHFUL WOMEN?
THEN, ONCE A YEAR FOR THE REST OF THEIR LIVES, THEY WOULD HAUL ALL THE LIMBLESS LADIES OUT IN THE TOWN SQUARE AND PELT THEM WITH GARBAGE.
THEY NEVER FORGAVE OR FORGOT!
WELL, IF YOU HATE HER SO MUCH, WHY DID YOU HIDE JUST NOW? WHY DIDN'T YOU SPIT IN HER EYE, OR SOMETHING?
OH, I GUESS I JUST DON'T WANT HER TO THINK THAT SHE BOTHERS ME. THE TRUTH IS THAT IF SHE ASKED I'D TAKE HER BACK IN A SECOND. I'M SO WEAK
LET'S GO HOME.
VIOLET, YOU'RE SO GOOD. YOU'LL NEVER LEAVE ME!
UH... OF COURSE NOT.*
GABBY GAMBOA

* YEAH...

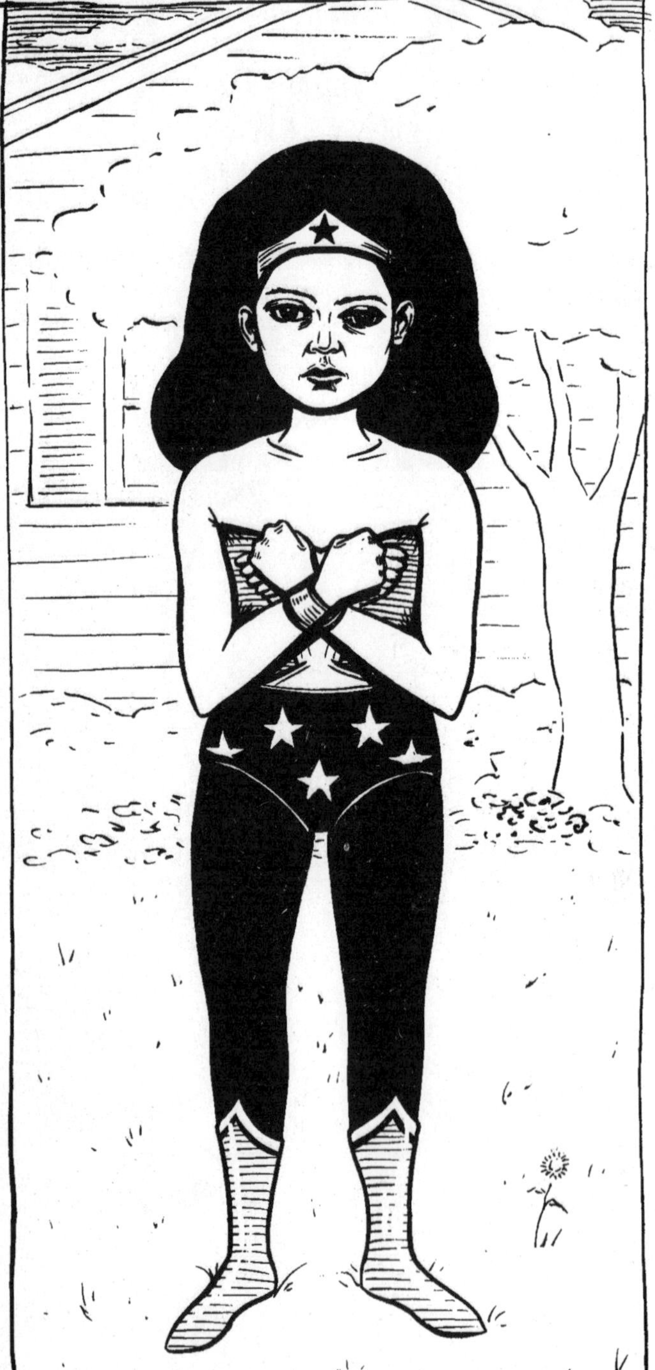
CHRISTINE SHIELDS

Wonder Woman is a trademark of D.C. Comics

I WAS A WANNABE WONDER WOMAN

All i can remember from my angst-ridden childhood is wanting to be powerful. To be able to wield the whip, to jump into my invisible plane and conquer the evildoers of the world, to deflect bullets from my gold-sheathed wrists. It could be me, i thought. I could be Wonder Woman. So, every day after school i headed out to the big oak tree in our front yard to begin my ritual. Spin, spin, spin... My arms crossed to my chest, i would twist my eleven year old body in the hope that maybe - if i concentrated hard enough - i would transform. My brain would teem with concentration... Change, change, change. At any moment my body would metamorphosize into that of a twentyfive year old sexpot, my hair would unfurl and flow to the gods, and i would know just whose ass to kick and exactly how to do it. It could happen.

Spin, spin, spin... i would keep going till inertia got the better of me, and then i would tumble onto the grass, too dizzy to know whether or not i had succeeded. Every time i kept my eyes sealed shut until i was a heap on the grass. And every time i cracked open my eyelids, i would stare at the sun, slowly shifting my gaze down to my body. Did it work? My heart would beat so hard. I was ready for the amazonian metamorphosis, i was ready to kick the asses of all those that deserved the dire fate of villains, i was truly ready to rule the world. But as soon as my eyes would catch the first glimpse of my bare grass-stained toes, i knew that it didn't work. I had failed, until the next time.

It wasn't only Wonder Woman who gave me hope for my little neurotic self, i was living in a dream world of super heroes and Sid & Marty Kroftisms.

I became deeply infatuated with Sigmund the Sea Monster. He was stepped on by his evil stepbrothers, always hiding from the outside world. Abused and tortured, Sigmund was a true romantic hero. His only refuge was the secret club-house of a kind neighbor boy who couldn't get anyone to believe that his best friend was a manic-depressive blubbery green sea monster. I could really relate to that somehow. I think that Sigmund was my first real crush. I just wanted to take him into my secret world and let him know that i would protect him from those dastardly brothers of his. I think Sigmund had a bit of a Cinderella complex.

Without Sid and Marty Kroft or Wonder Woman, i would have been barren of the sur-reality that greased the gears of my torturously slow adolescence. On the Kroft Superstars, all of the characters were just ordinary kids in extraordinarily twisted situations. The Bugaloos flitted around evading evil while playing in a jamming rock band. Jimmy on H.R. Puf 'n Stuf was constantly trying to figure out just how the fuck he landed on that magic island, while cleverly fighting off that nasty Witchypoo with the help of his magic flute. The (original) Land of the Lost, Dr. Shrinker, Electra Woman and Dyna Girl....

All of these shows provided me with an escape route from banality. They taught me to fight evil by tapping the rich well of my burgeoning preteen imagination. They taught me that i could do anything if i just concentrated hard enough.

Words by Alicia Rose

Picture by Christine Shields

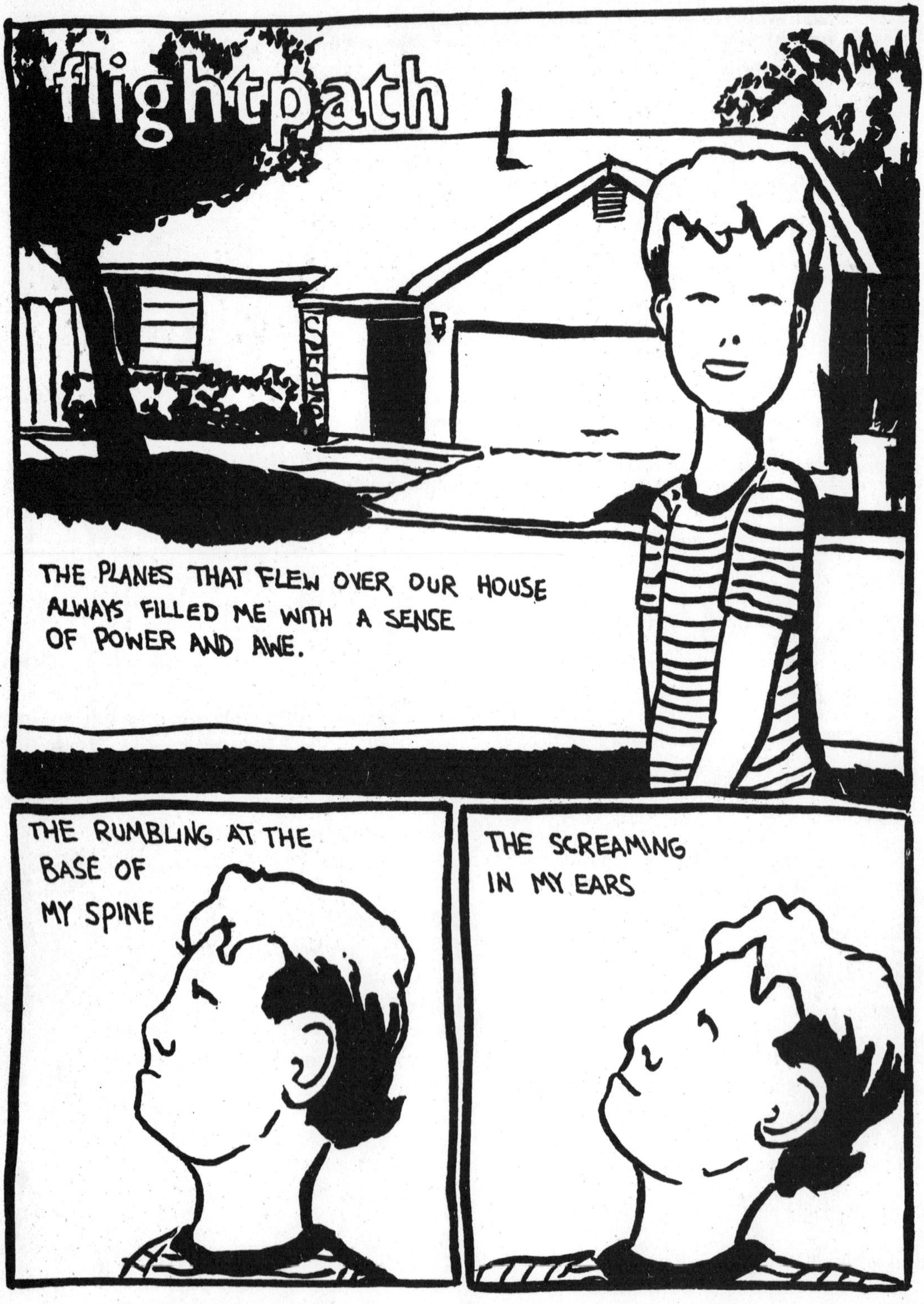
flightpath
THE PLANES THAT FLEW OVER OUR HOUSE ALWAYS FILLED ME WITH A SENSE OF POWER AND AWE.
THE RUMBLING AT THE BASE OF MY SPINE
THE SCREAMING IN MY EARS

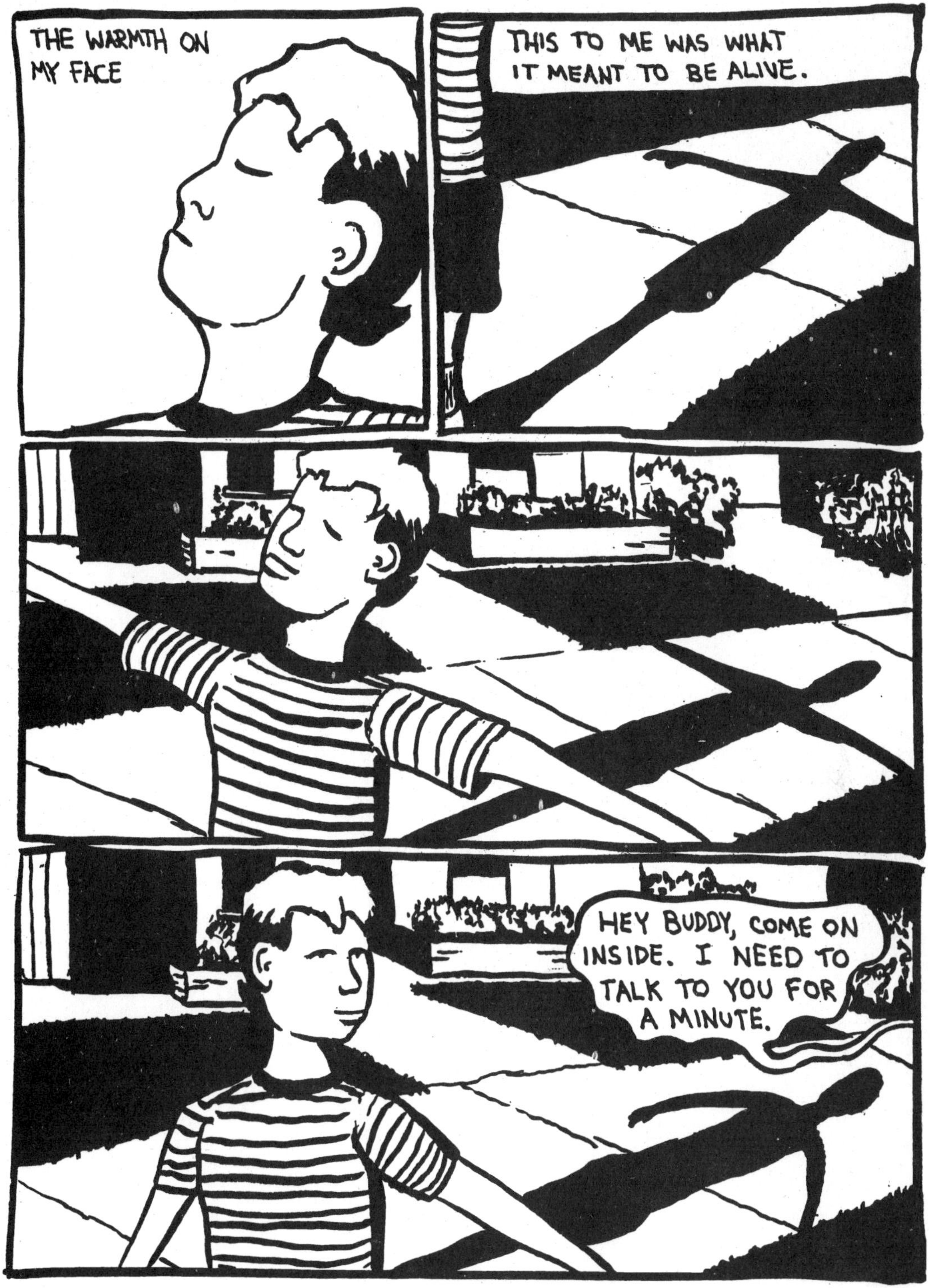
THE WARMTH ON MY FACE
THIS TO ME WAS WHAT IT MEANT TO BE ALIVE.
HEY BUDDY, COME ON INSIDE. I NEED TO TALK TO YOU FOR A MINUTE.

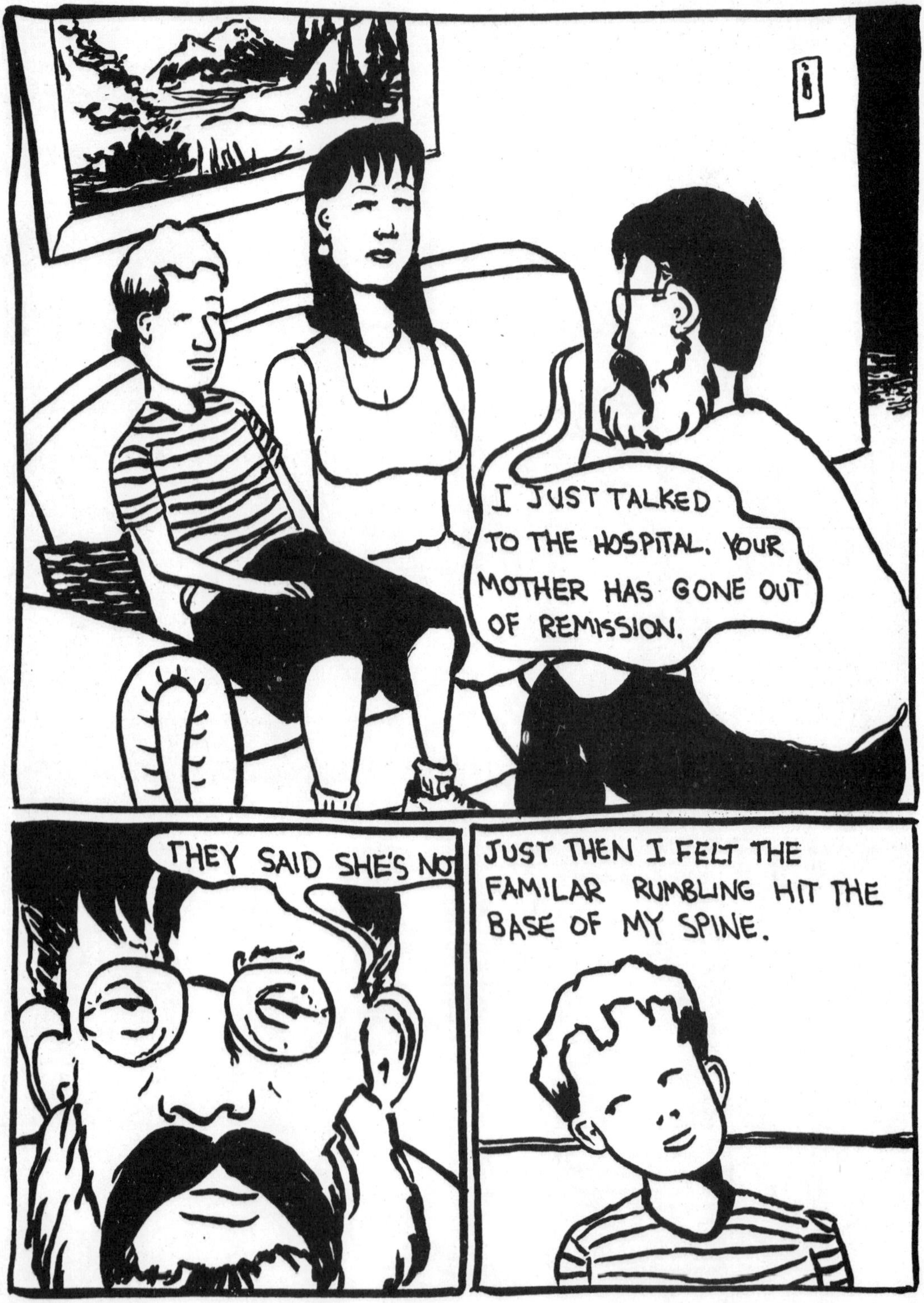
I JUST TALKED TO THE HOSPITAL. YOUR MOTHER HAS GONE OUT OF REMISSION.
THEY SAID SHE'S NOT
JUST THEN I FELT THE FAMILAR RUMBLING HIT THE BASE OF MY SPINE.

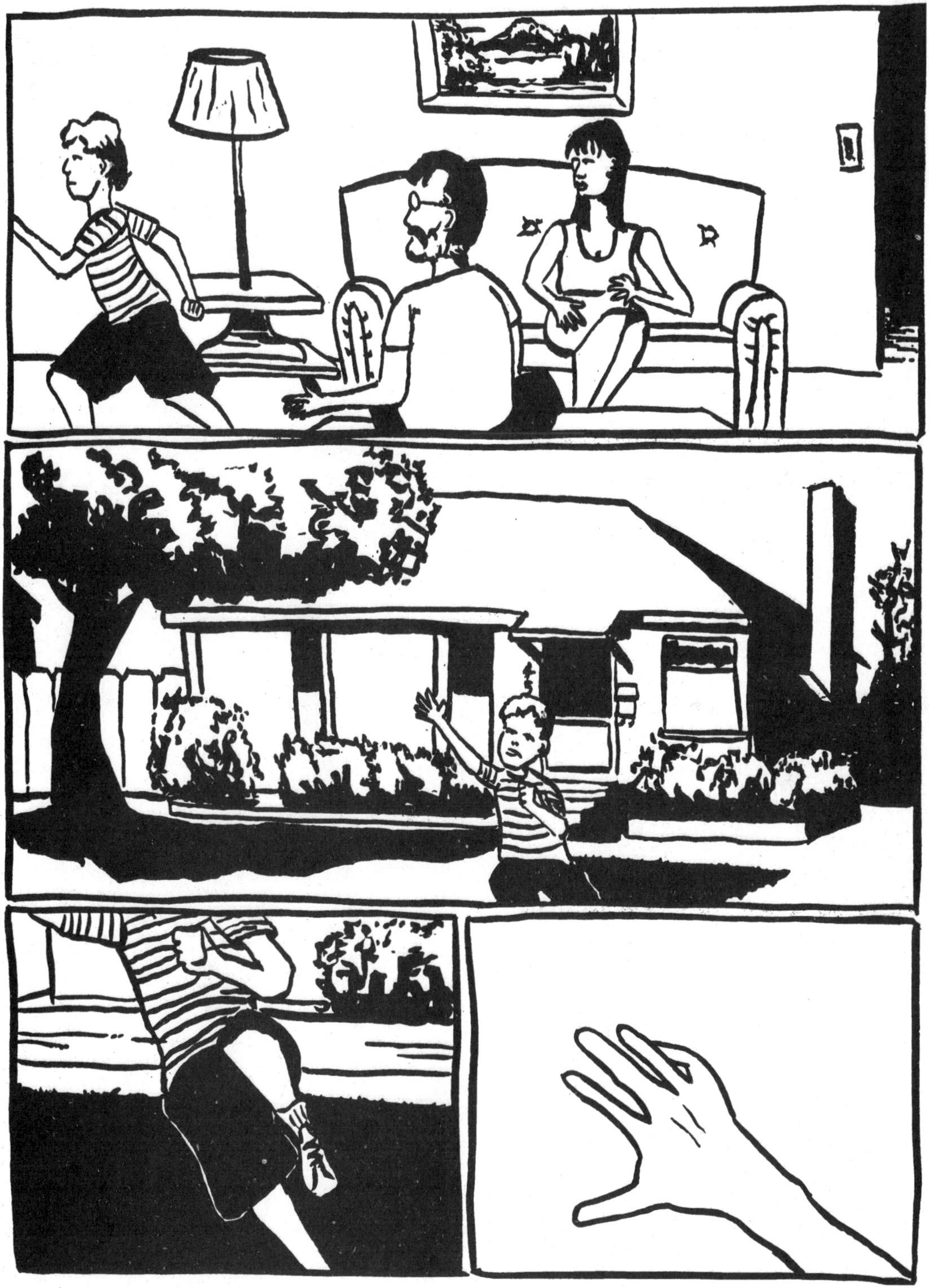

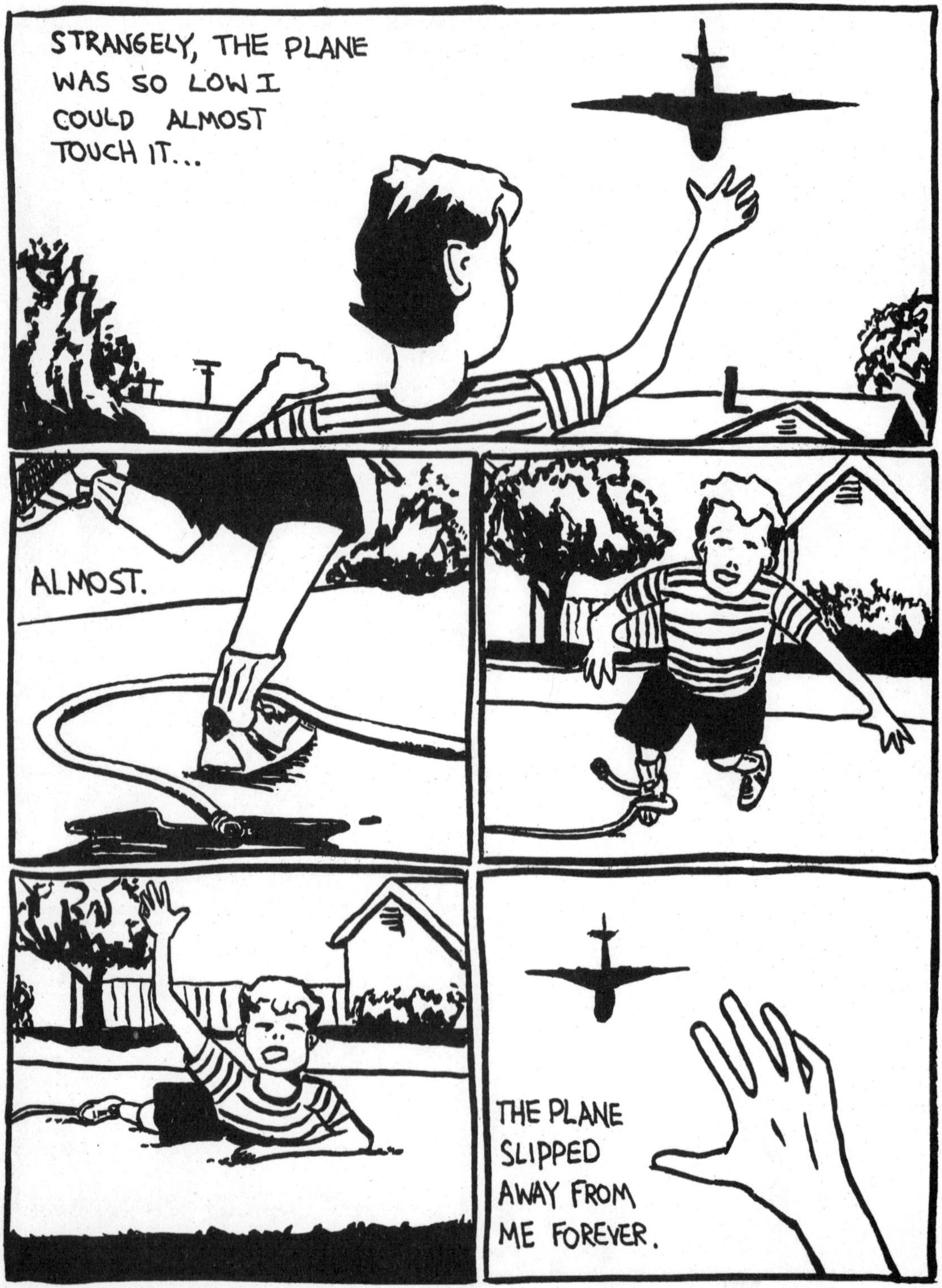
STRANGELY, THE PLANE WAS SO LOW I COULD ALMOST TOUCH IT...
ALMOST.
THE PLANE SLIPPED AWAY FROM ME FOREVER.

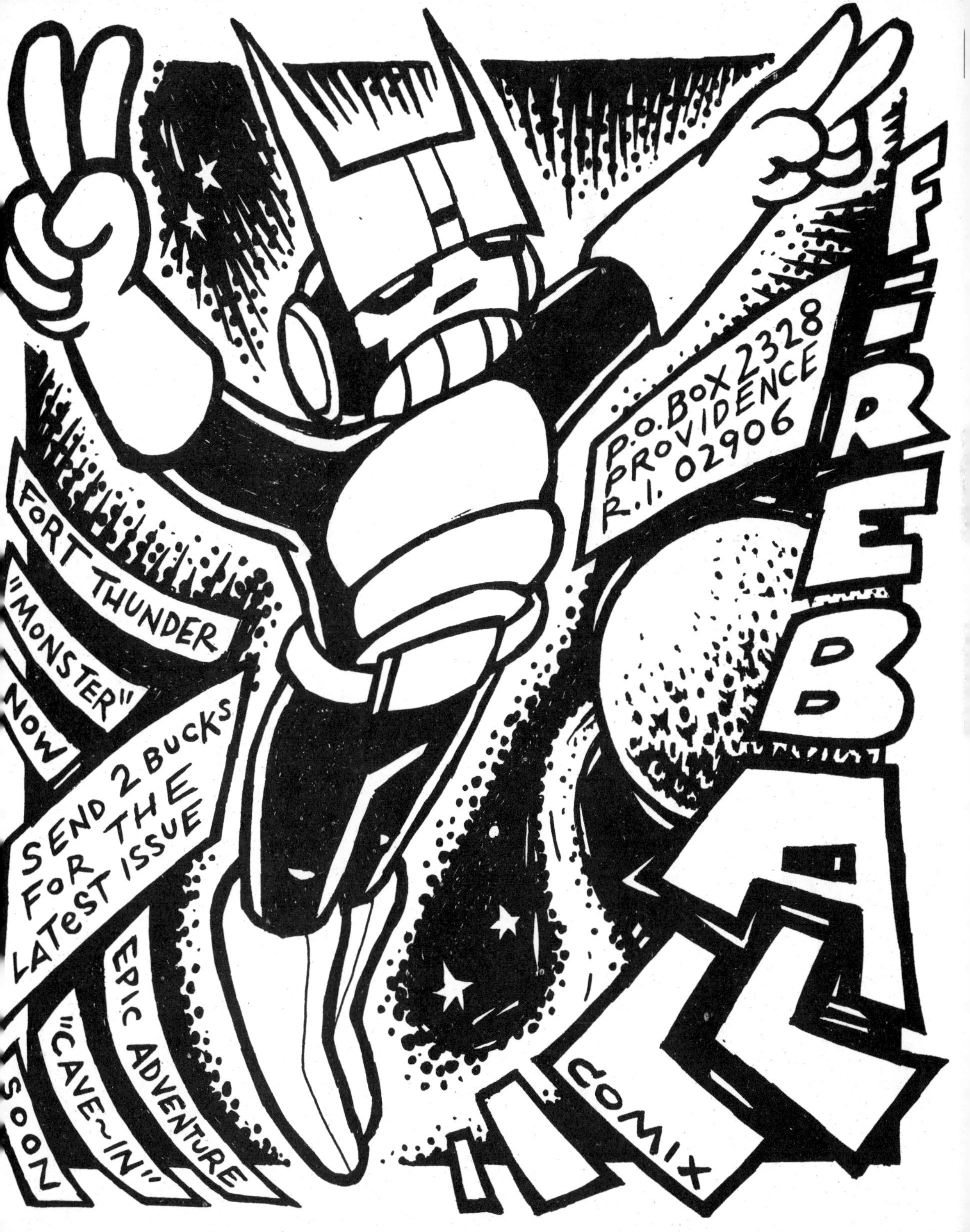
FIREBALL
P.O. BOX 2328
PROVIDENCE
R.I. 02906
FORT THUNDER
"MONSTER"
NOW
SEND 2 BUCKS
FOR THE
LATEST ISSUE
EPIC ADVENTURE
"CAVE~IN"
SOON
COMIX

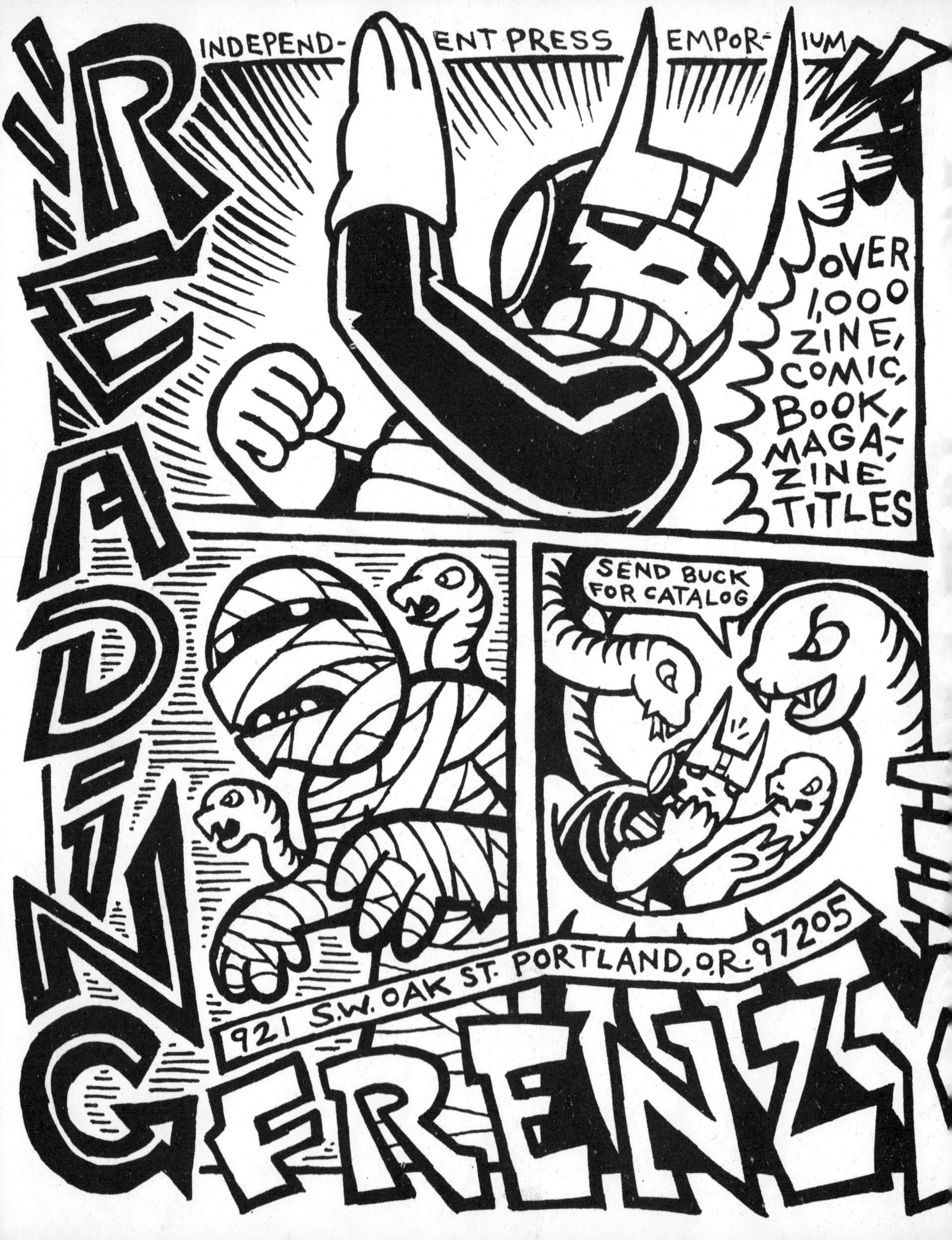

READING
INDEPENDENT PRESS EMPORIUM
OVER 1,000 ZINE/COMIC/BOOK/MAGAZINE TITLES
SEND BUCK FOR CATALOG
921 S.W. OAK ST. PORTLAND, O.R. 97205
FRENZY

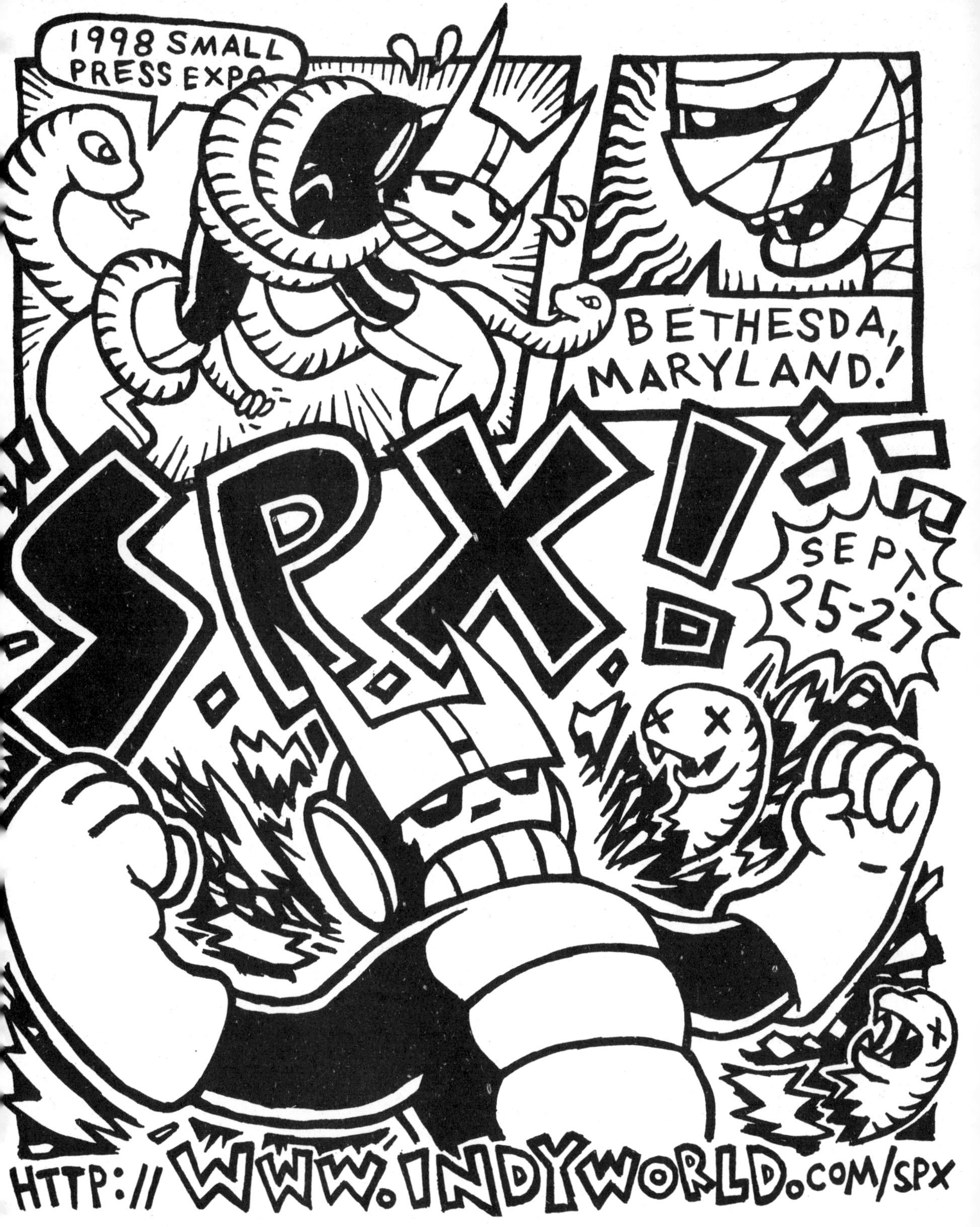
1998 SMALL PRESS EXPO
BETHESDA, MARYLAND!
SPX!
SEPT. 25-27
HTTP://WWW.INDYWORLD.COM/SPX

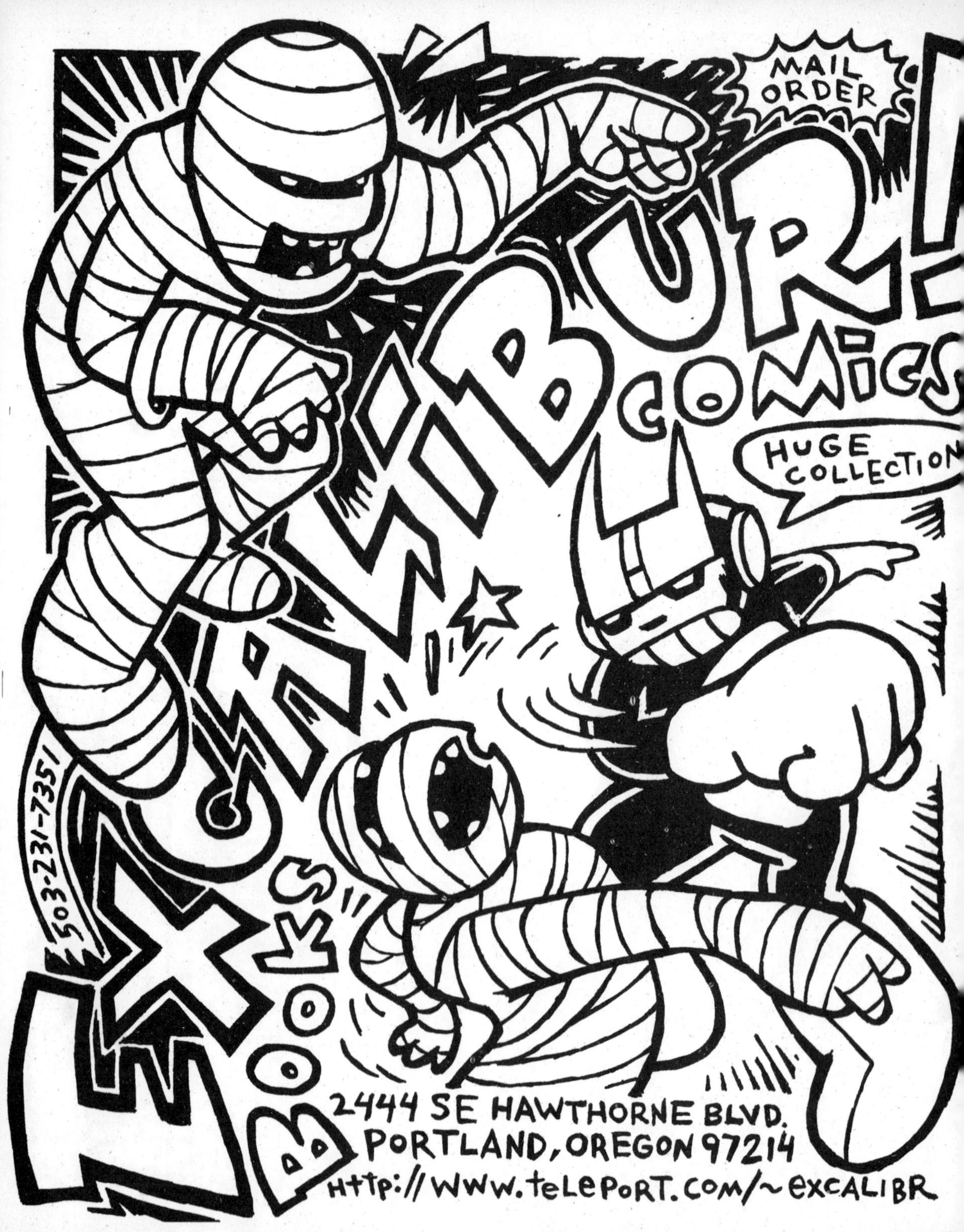
MAIL ORDER
EXCALIBUR!
COMICS
HUGE COLLECTION
BOOKS
503-231-7351
2444 SE HAWTHORNE BLVD.
PORTLAND, OREGON 97214
Http://www.teleport.com/~excalibr

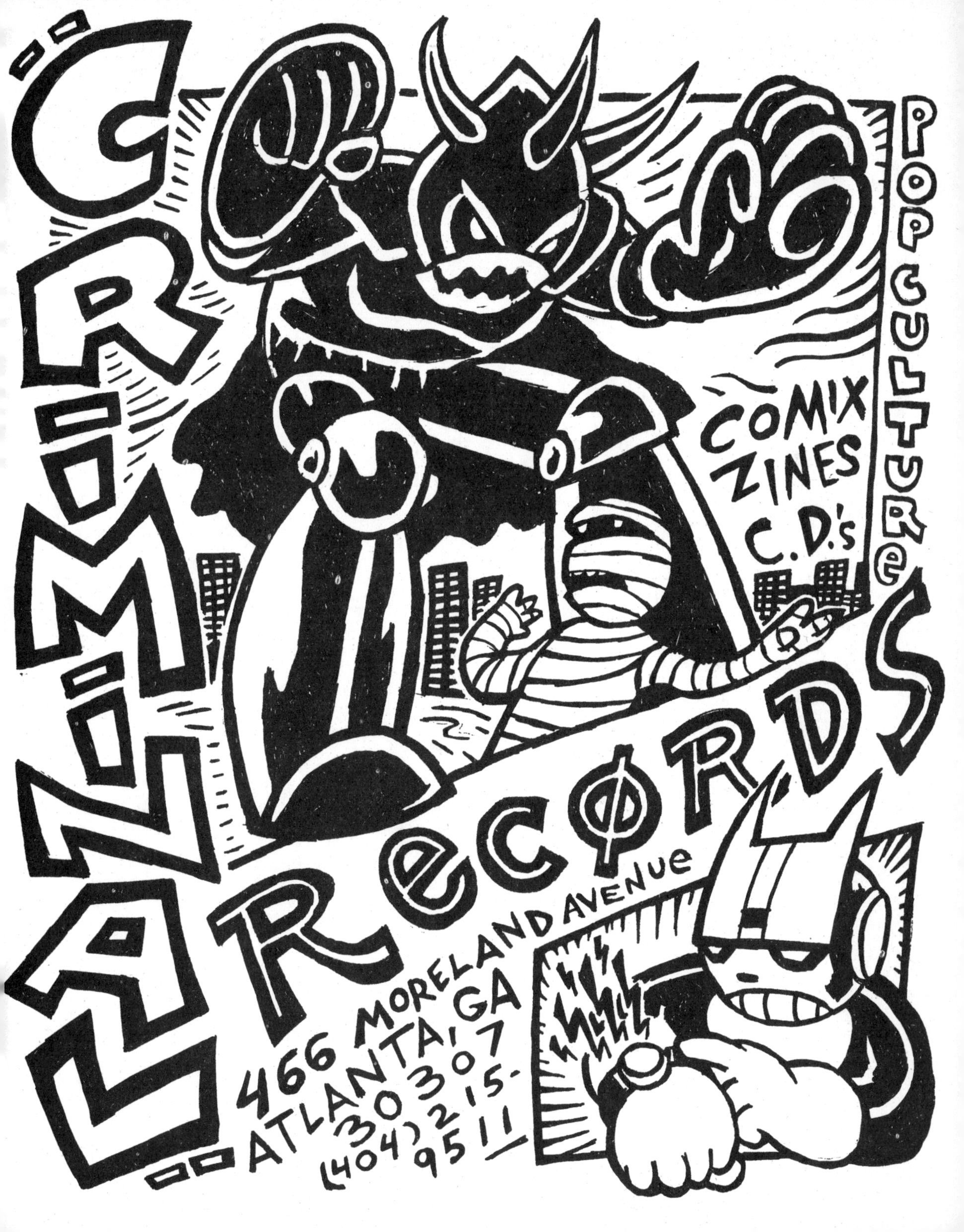
CRIMINAL
RECORDS
POP CULTURE
COMIX
ZINES
C.D.'s
466 MORELAND AVENUE
ATLANTA, GA
30307
(404) 215-9511

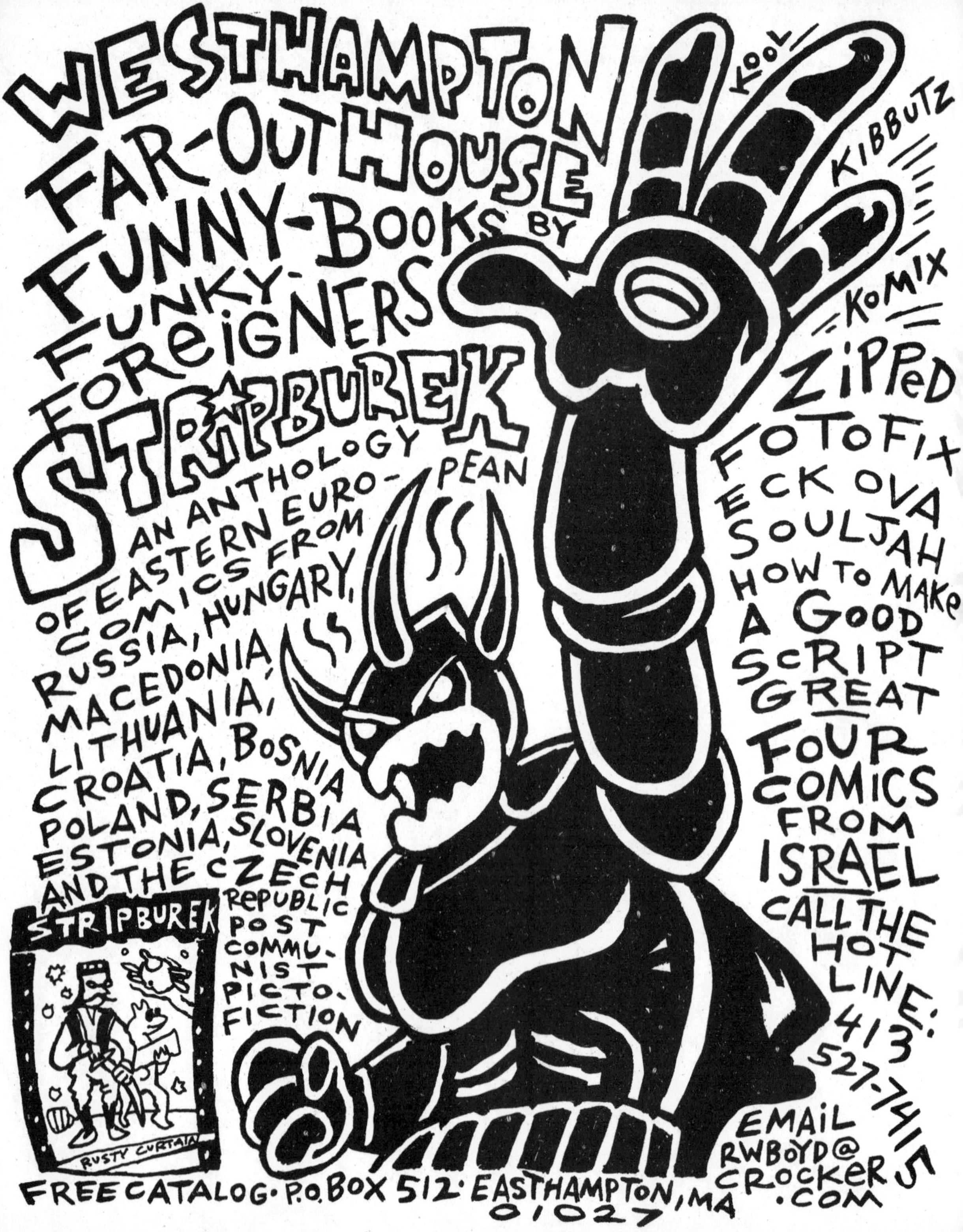
WESTHAMPTON
FAR-OUTHOUSE
FUNNY-BOOKS BY
FUNKY-
FOREIGNERS
STRIPBUREK
AN ANTHOLOGY OF EASTERN EURO-PEAN COMICS FROM RUSSIA, HUNGARY, MACEDONIA, LITHUANIA, CROATIA, BOSNIA POLAND, SERBIA ESTONIA, SLOVENIA AND THE CZECH REPUBLIC
POST COMMUNIST PICTO-FICTION
STRIPBUREK
RUSTY CURTAIN
KOOL KIBBUTZ KOMIX
ZIPPED FOTOFIX ECKOVA SOULJAH HOW TO MAKE A GOOD SCRIPT GREAT
FOUR COMICS FROM ISRAEL
CALL THE HOT LINE: 413 527-7415
EMAIL RWBOYD@CROCKER.COM
FREE CATALOG · P.O. BOX 512 · EASTHAMPTON, MA 01027

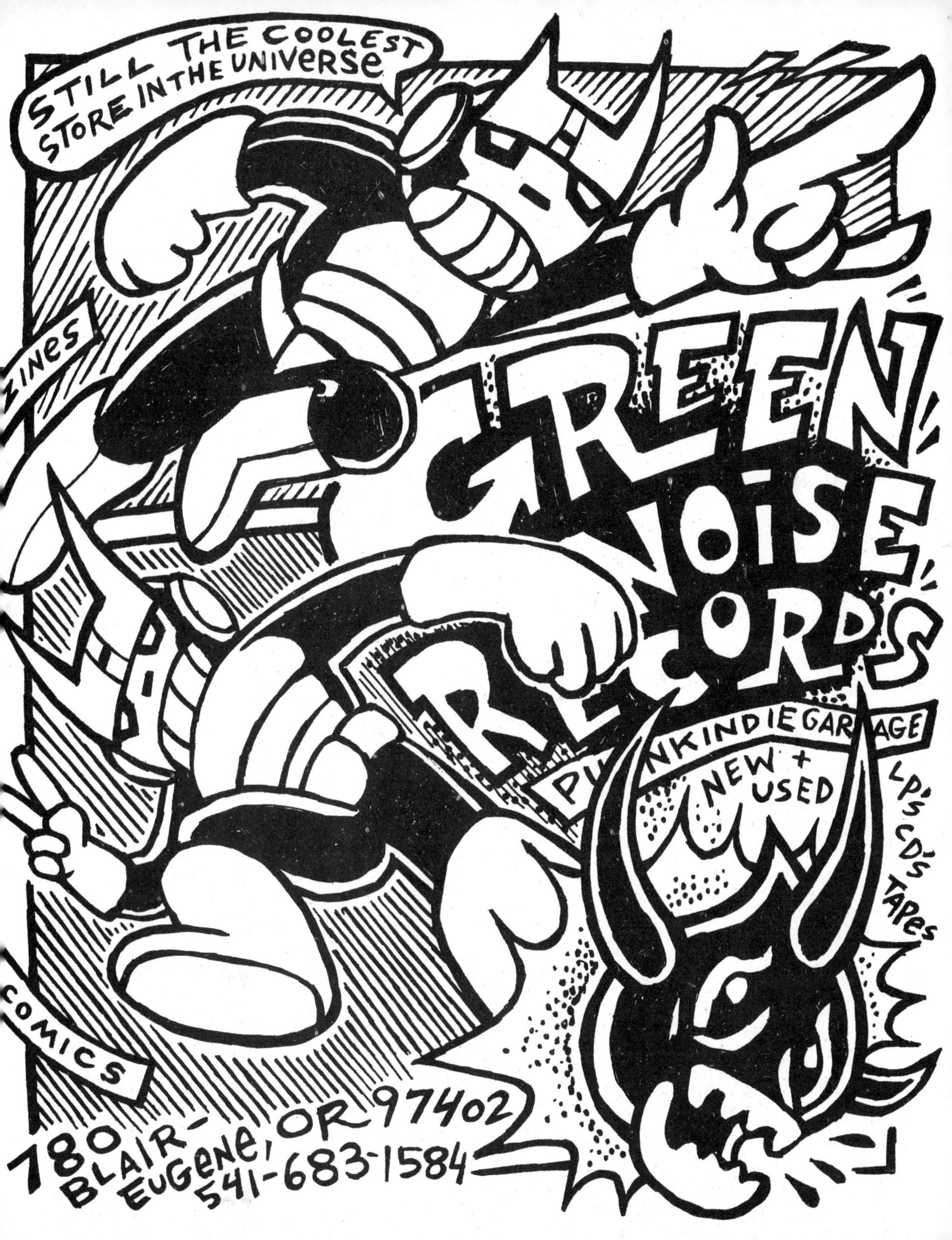
STILL THE COOLEST STORE IN THE UNIVERSE
ZINES
GREEN NOISE RECORDS
PUNK INDIE GARAGE
NEW + USED
LP'S CD'S TAPES
COMICS
780 BLAIR - EUGENE, OR 97402
541-683-1584

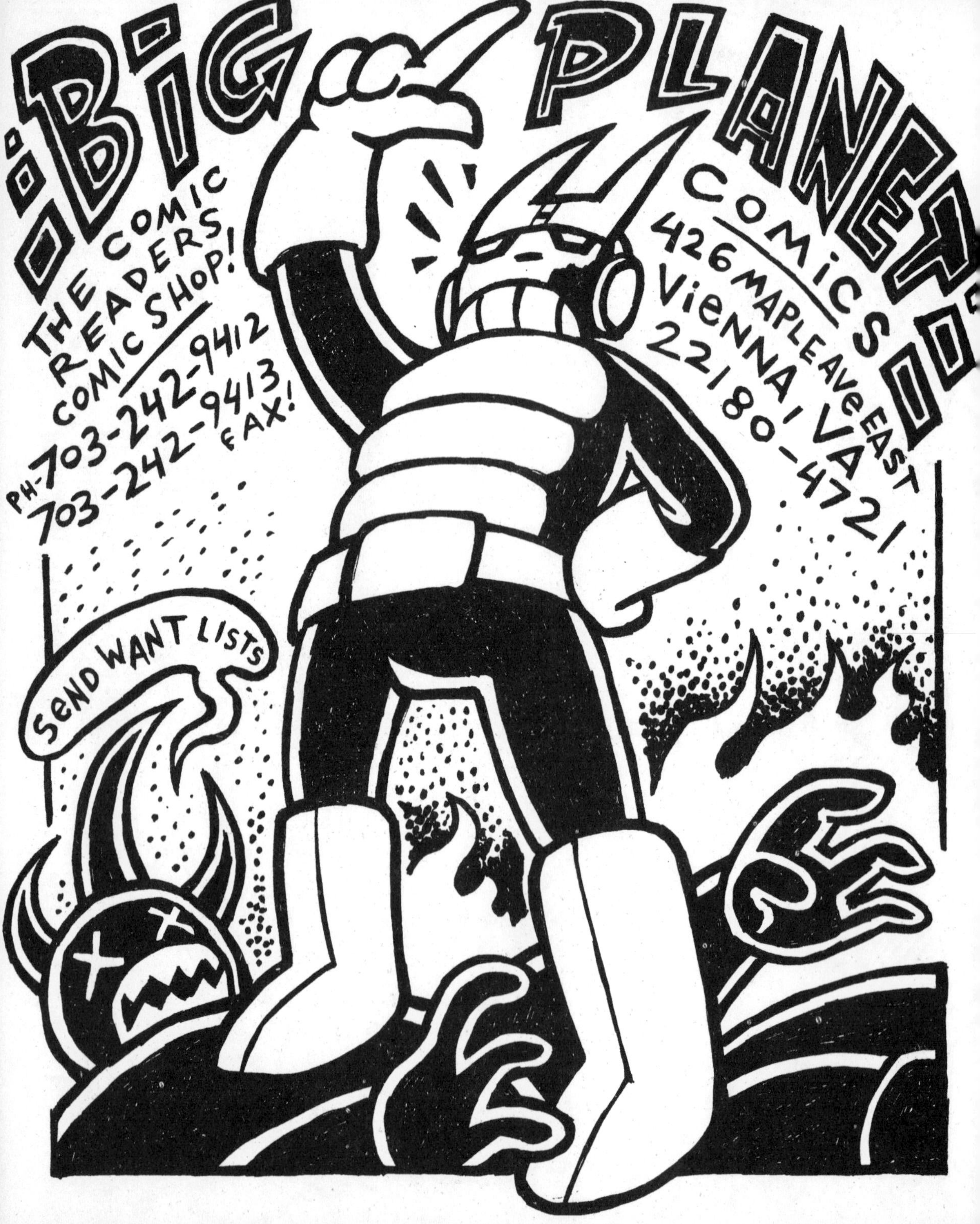

BIG PLANET
COMICS
THE COMIC READERS COMIC SHOP!
PH-703-242-9412
703-242-9413 FAX!
426 MAPLE AVE EAST
VIENNA, VA
22180-4721
SEND WANT LISTS

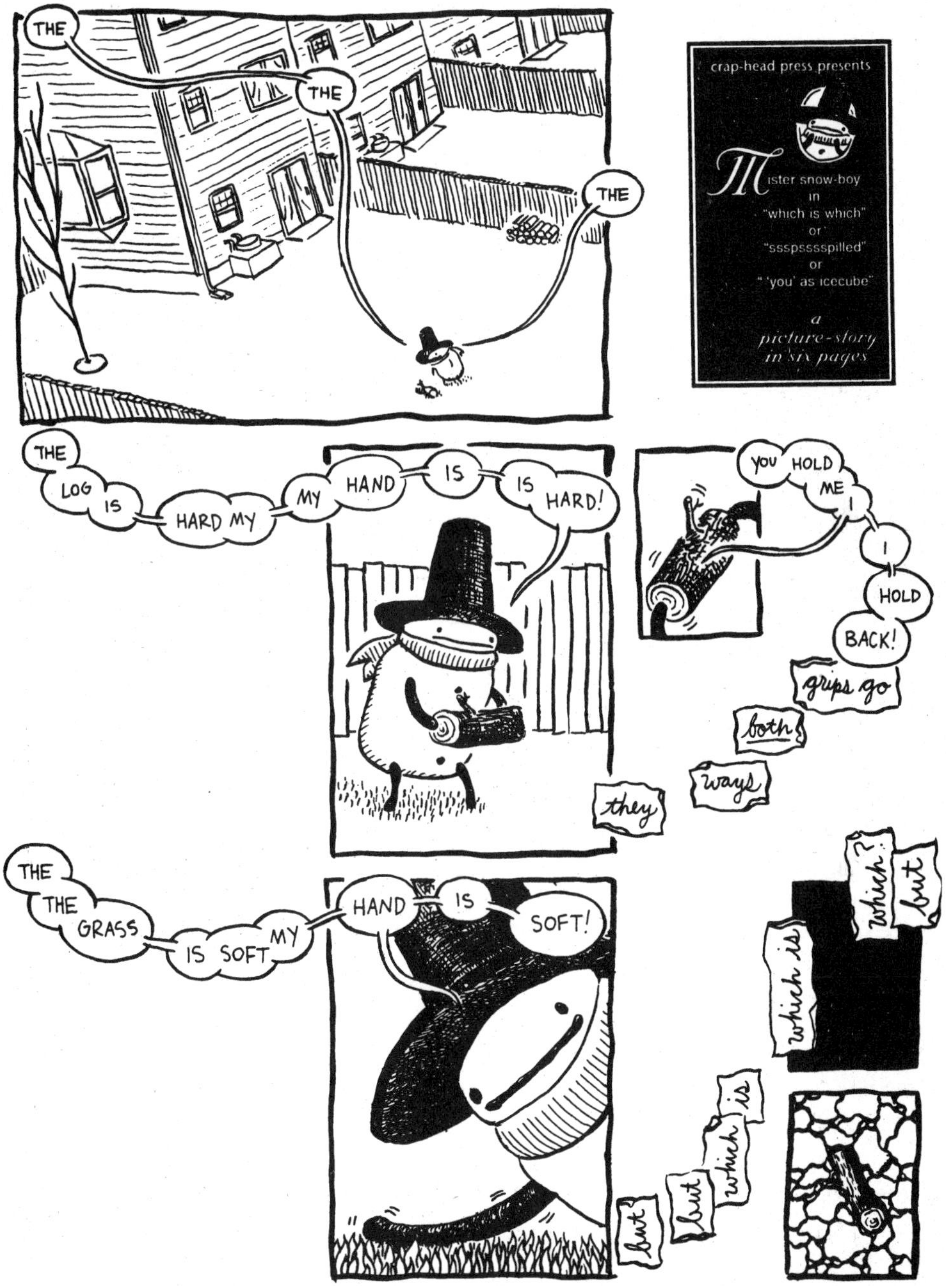
THE
THE
THE
crap-head press presents
Mister snow-boy
in
"which is which"
or
"ssspssssspilled"
or
" 'you' as icecube"
a
picture-story
in six pages
THE
LOG
IS
HARD MY
MY
HAND
IS
IS
HARD!
YOU
HOLD
ME
I
I
HOLD
BACK!
grips go
both
ways
they
THE
THE
GRASS
IS SOFT
MY
HAND
IS
SOFT!
but
which?
which is
which
is
but
but

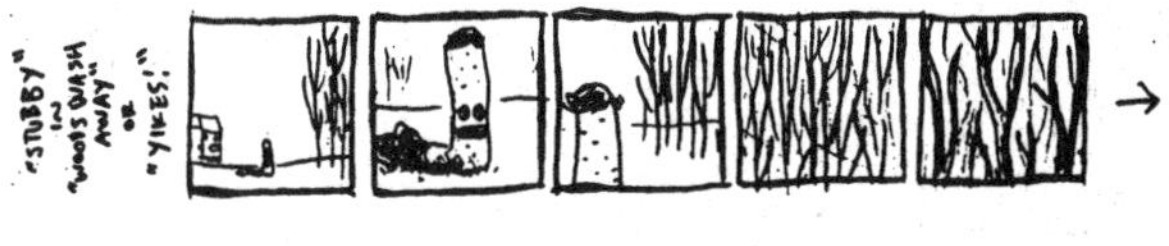
"STUBBY"
in
"WOODS WASH AWAY"
or
"YIKES!"
hi!
→

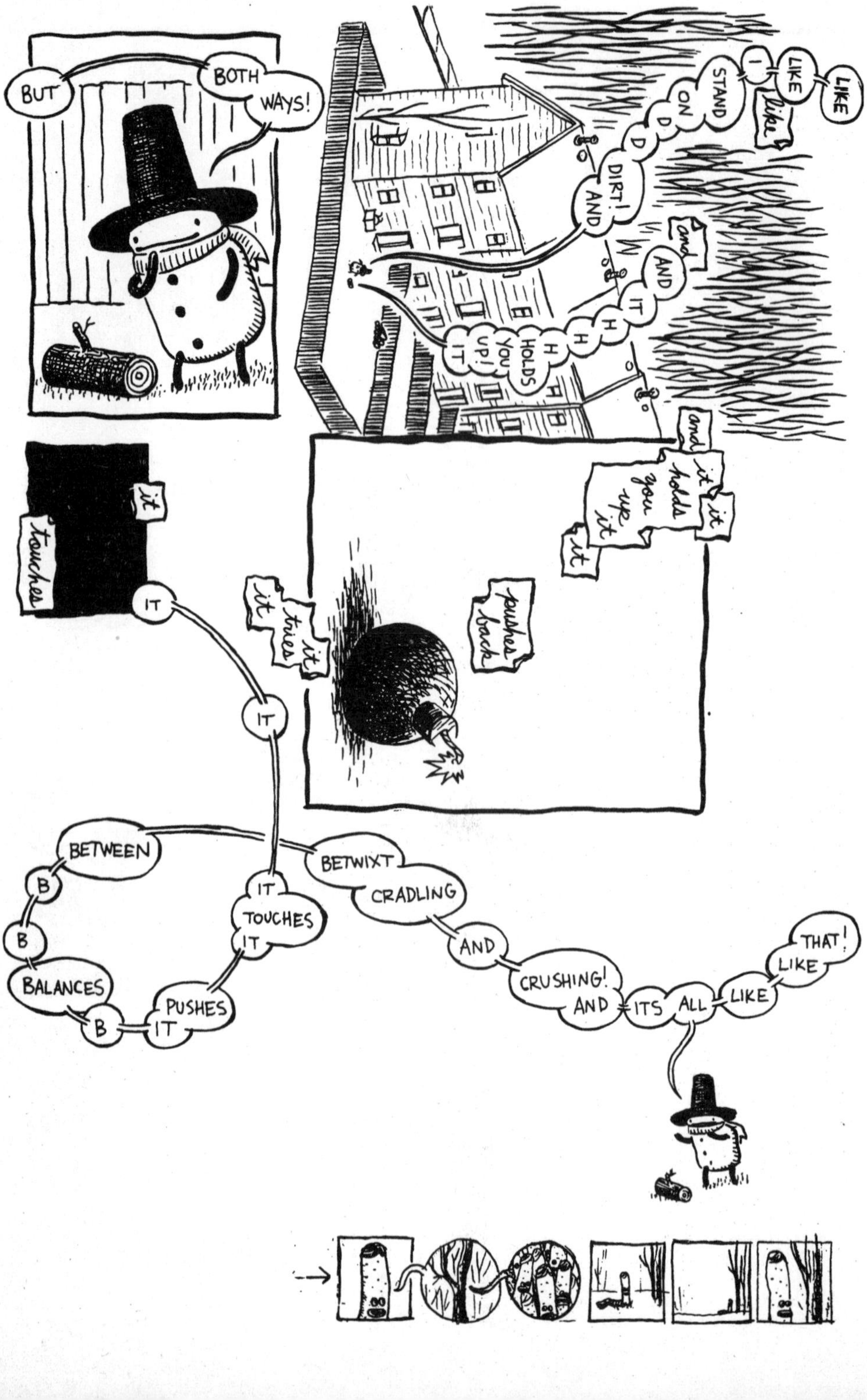

BUT
BOTH
WAYS!
LIKE
LIKE
like
I
STAND
ON
D
D
DIRT!
AND
AND
and
IT
H
H
H
HOLDS
YOU
UP!
IT
and
it
holds
you
up
it
it
it
it
touches
IT
it
tries
it
it
pushes
back
IT
BETWEEN
B
B
BALANCES
B
IT
PUSHES
IT
TOUCHES
IT
BETWIXT
CRADLING
AND
CRUSHING!
AND
ITS
ALL
LIKE
LIKE
THAT!

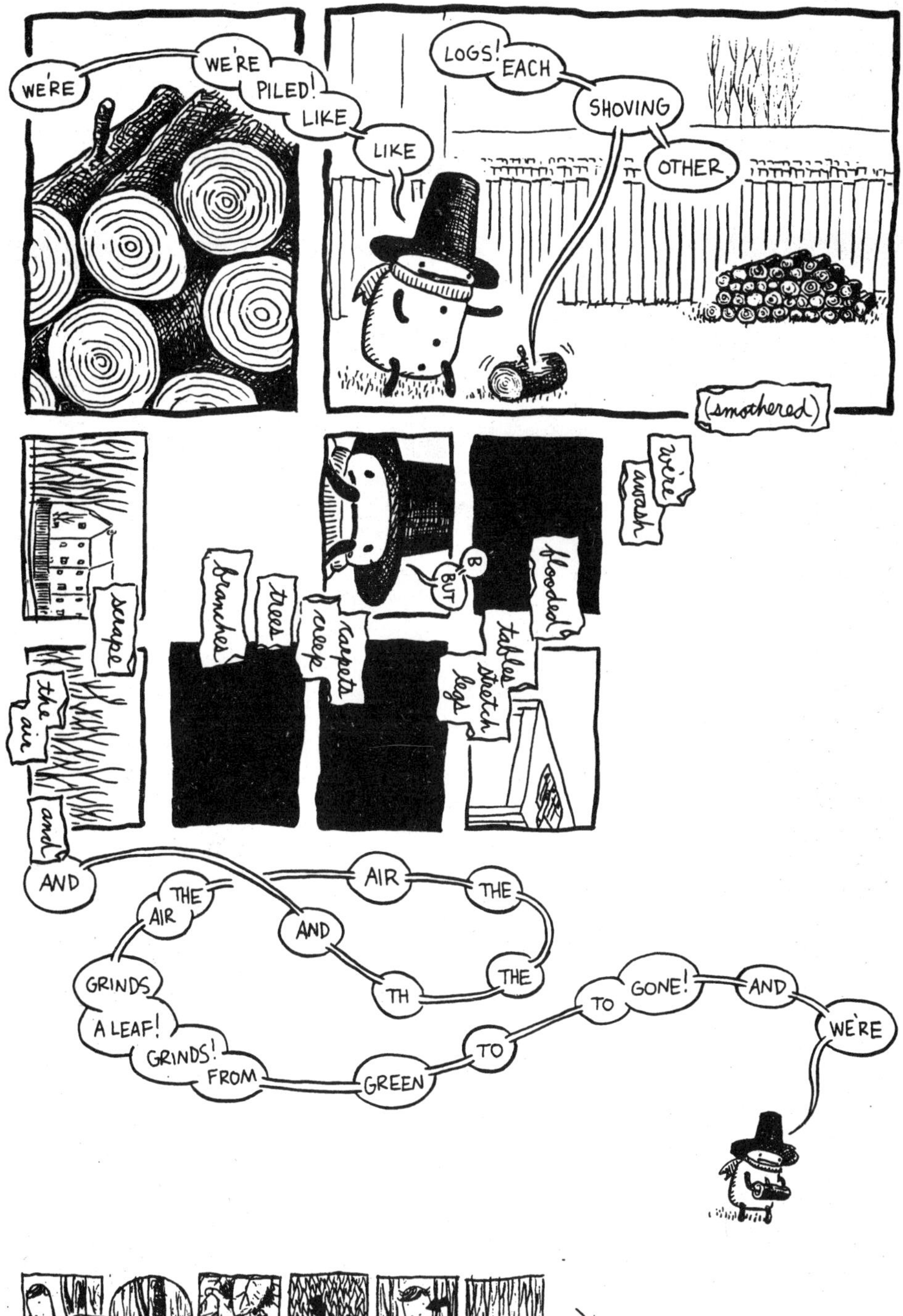

WE'RE
WE'RE
PILED!
LIKE
LIKE
LOGS!
EACH
SHOVING
OTHER
(smothered)
we're
awash
B
BUT
flooded
tables
stretch
legs
carpets
creep
trees
branches
scape
the
air
and
AND
THE
AIR
AND
AIR
THE
THE
TH
GRINDS
A LEAF!
GRINDS!
FROM
GREEN
TO
TO
GONE!
AND
WE'RE

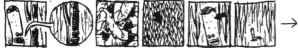

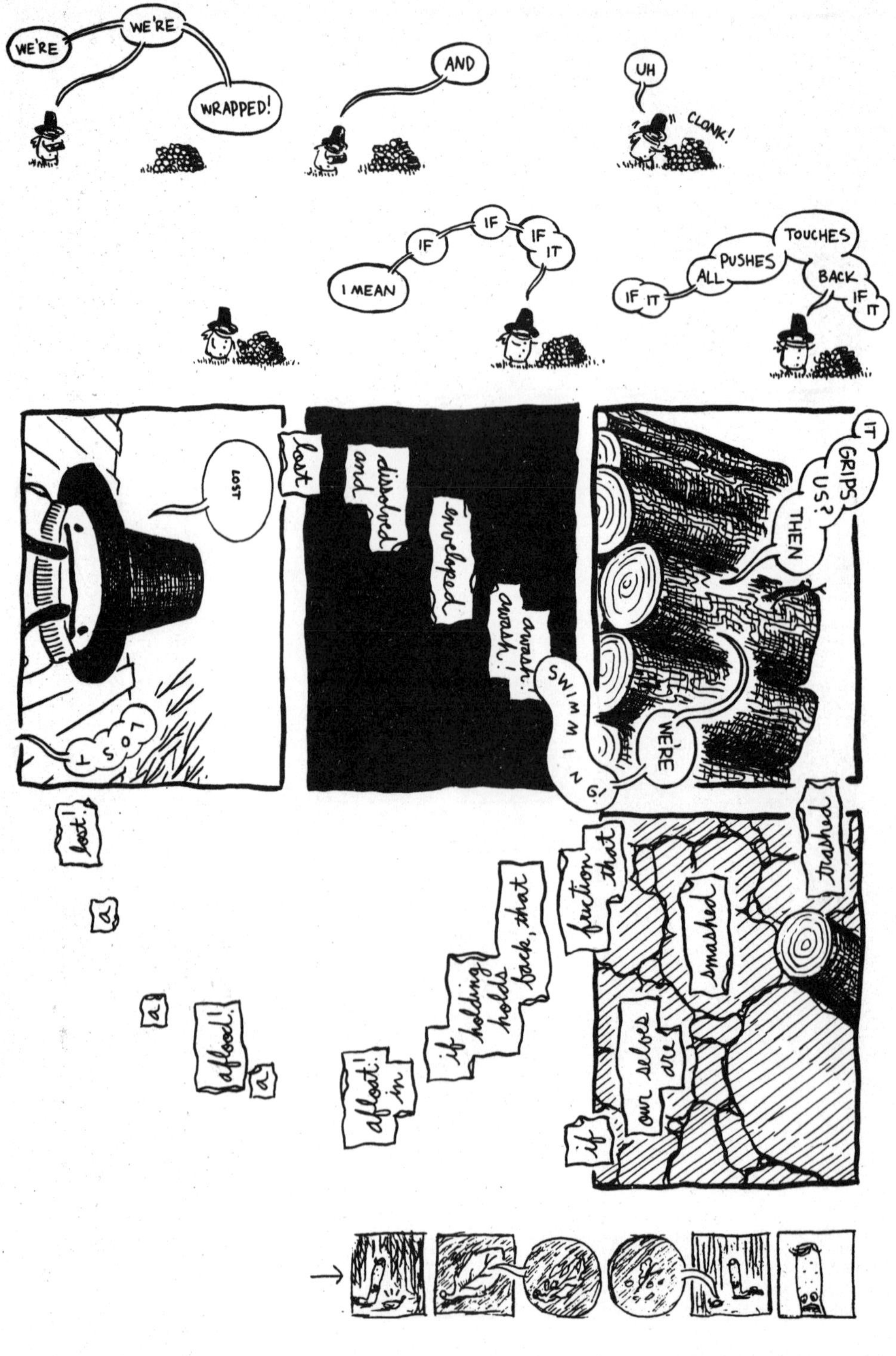
WE'RE
WE'RE
WRAPPED!
AND
UH
CLONK!
I MEAN
IF
IF
IF IT
IF IT
ALL
PUSHES
TOUCHES
BACK
IF IT
lost
LOST
L O S T
dissolved and
enveloped
awash... awash!
SWIMMING!
WE'RE
IT GRIPS US? THEN
lost!
a
a
afloat!
a
afloat! in
if holding holds back, that
friction that
smashed
trashed
if
our selves are

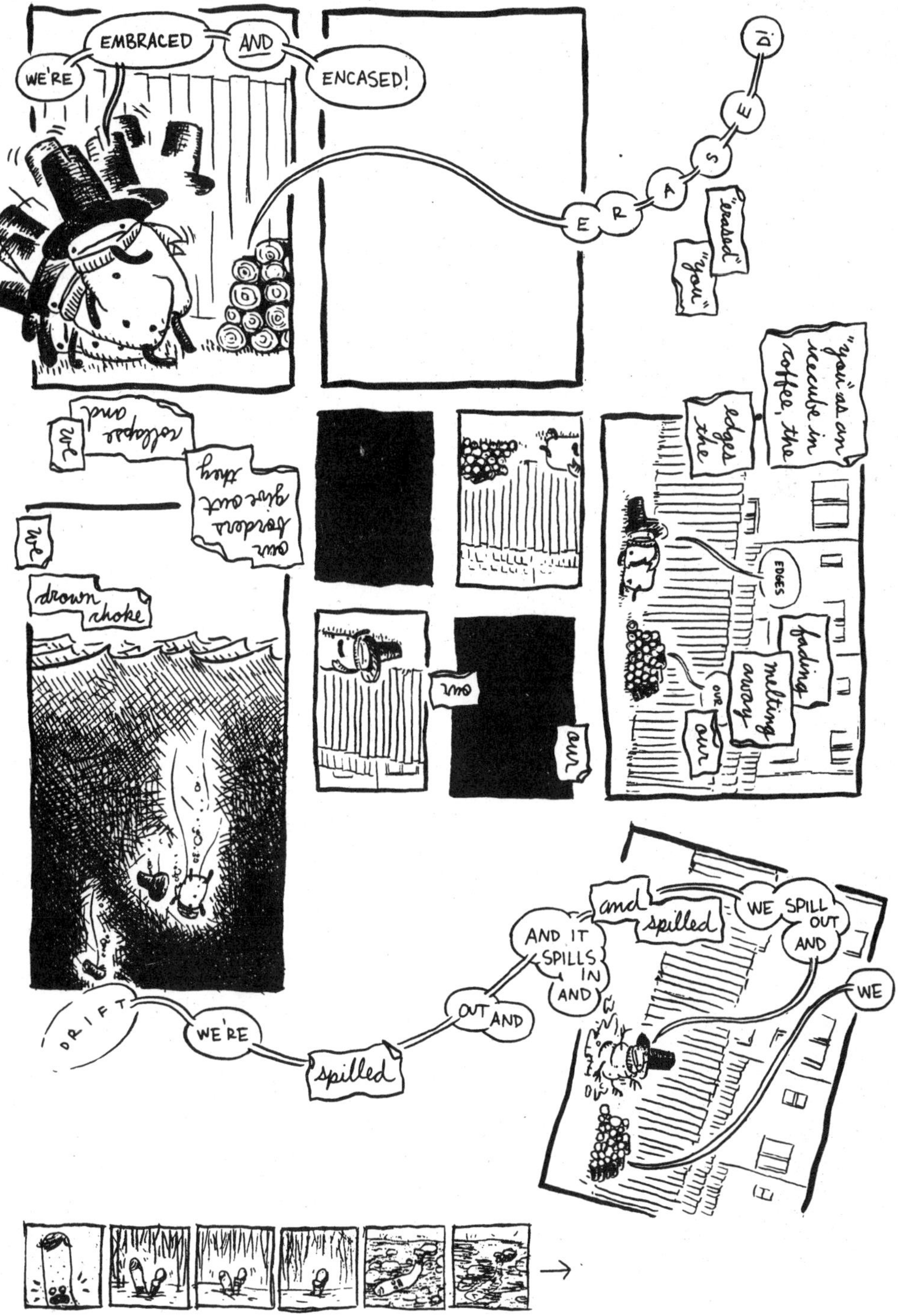

WE'RE
EMBRACED
AND
ENCASED!
ERASED!
"erased"
"you"
"you" as an icecube in coffee, the
edges the
EDGES
fading
melting away
OUR
air
our
our
we
collapse and
our borders give out they
we
drown
choke
DRIFT
WE'RE
spilled
OUT AND
AND IT SPILLS IN AND
and
spilled
WE SPILL OUT AND
WE

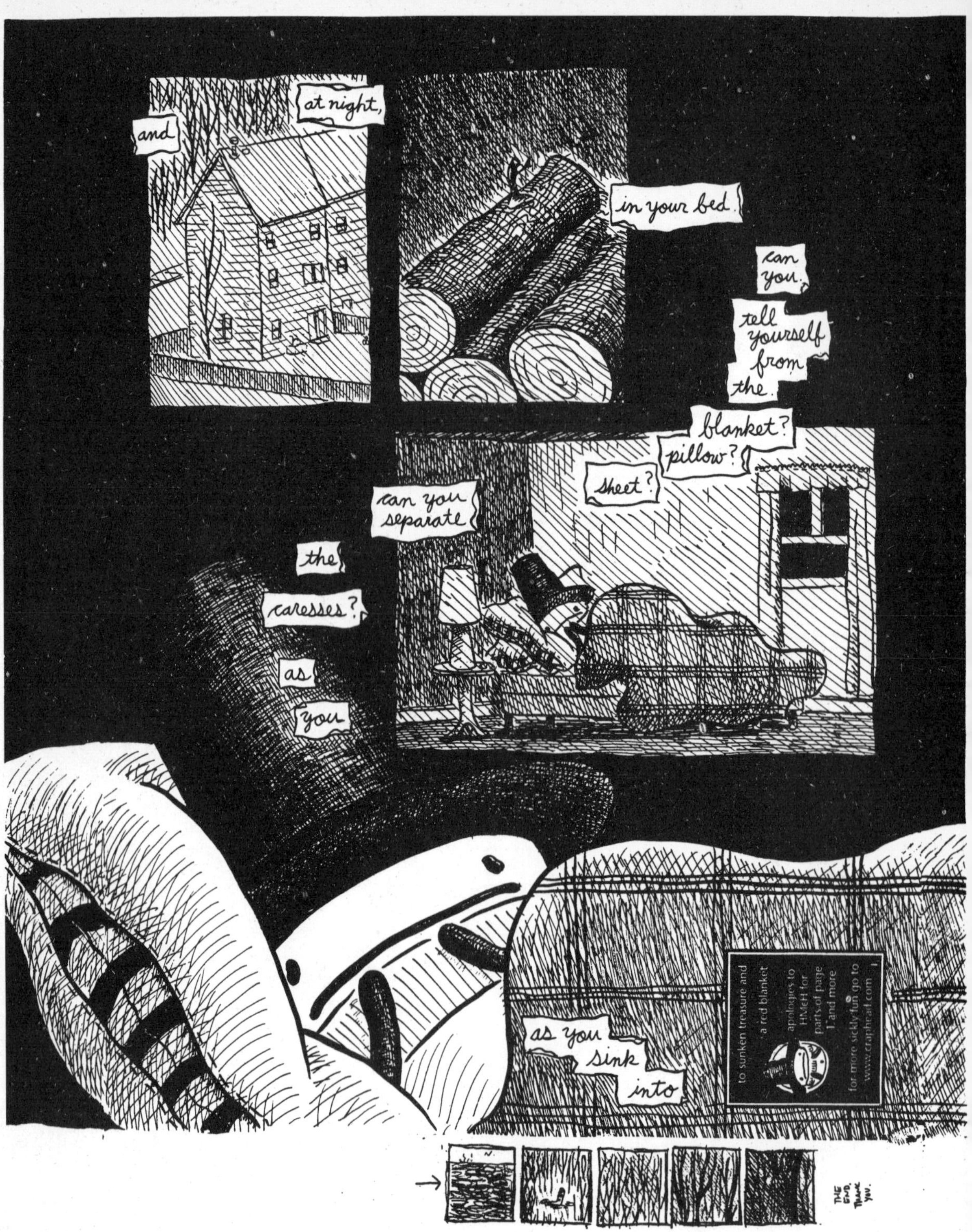

and
at night,
in your bed
can you
tell yourself from the
blanket?
pillow?
sheet?
can you separate
the
caresses?
as
you
as you sink into
to sunken treasure and a red blanket
apologies to HMeH for parts of page 1 and more
for more sickly fun go to www.craphead.com
THE END. THANK YOU.

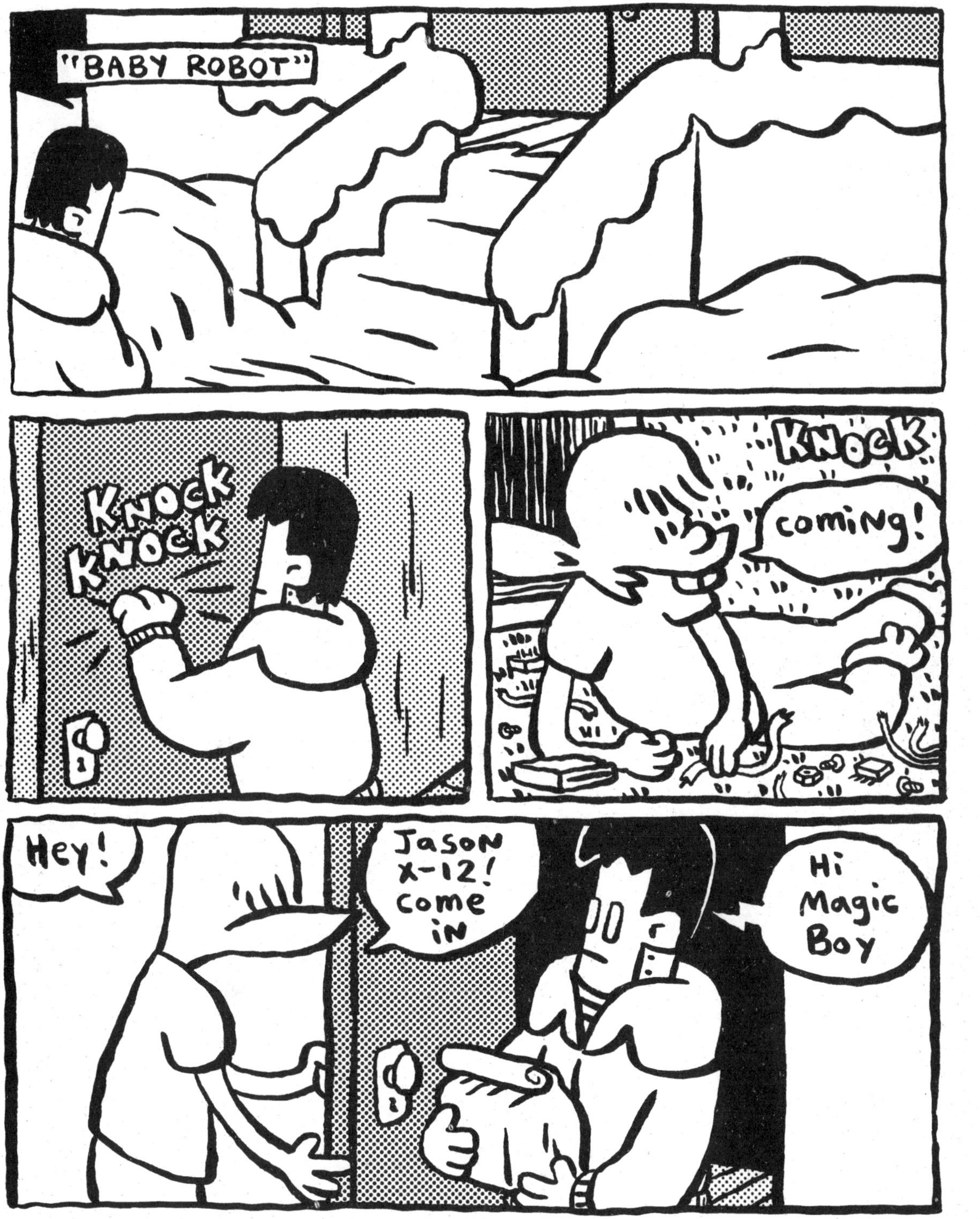
"BABY ROBOT"
KNOCK KNOCK
KNOCK
coming!
Hey!
Jason X-12! come in
Hi Magic Boy

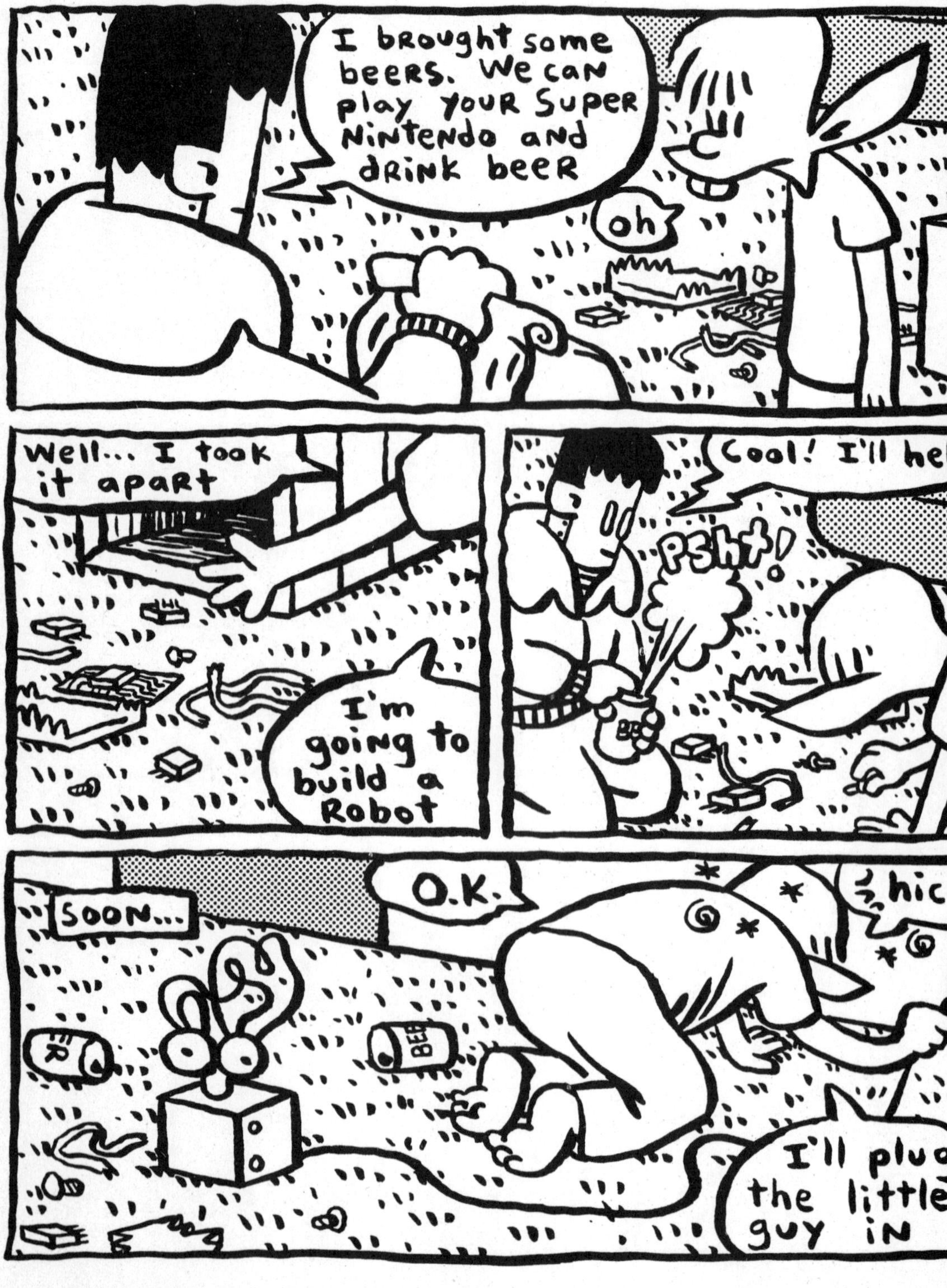
I brought some beers. We can play your Super Nintendo and drink beer
oh
Well... I took it apart
I'm going to build a Robot
Cool! I'll help
PSHT!
SOON...
O.K.
hic
I'll plug the little guy in

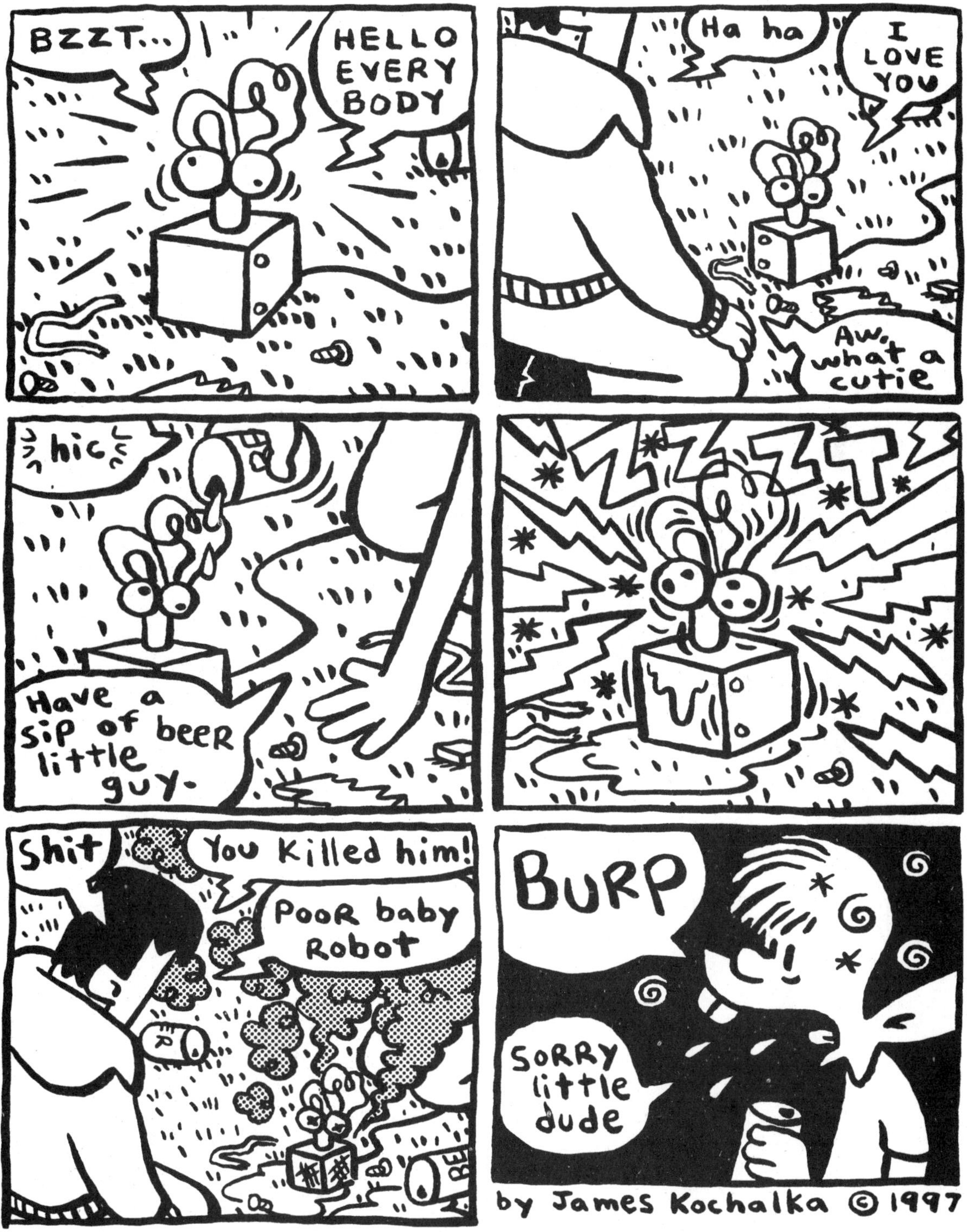
BZZT...
HELLO EVERY BODY
Ha ha
I LOVE YOU
Aw, what a cutie
hic
Have a sip of beer little guy.
ZZZT
Shit
You killed him!
POOR baby Robot
BURP
SORRY little dude

by James Kochalka © 1997

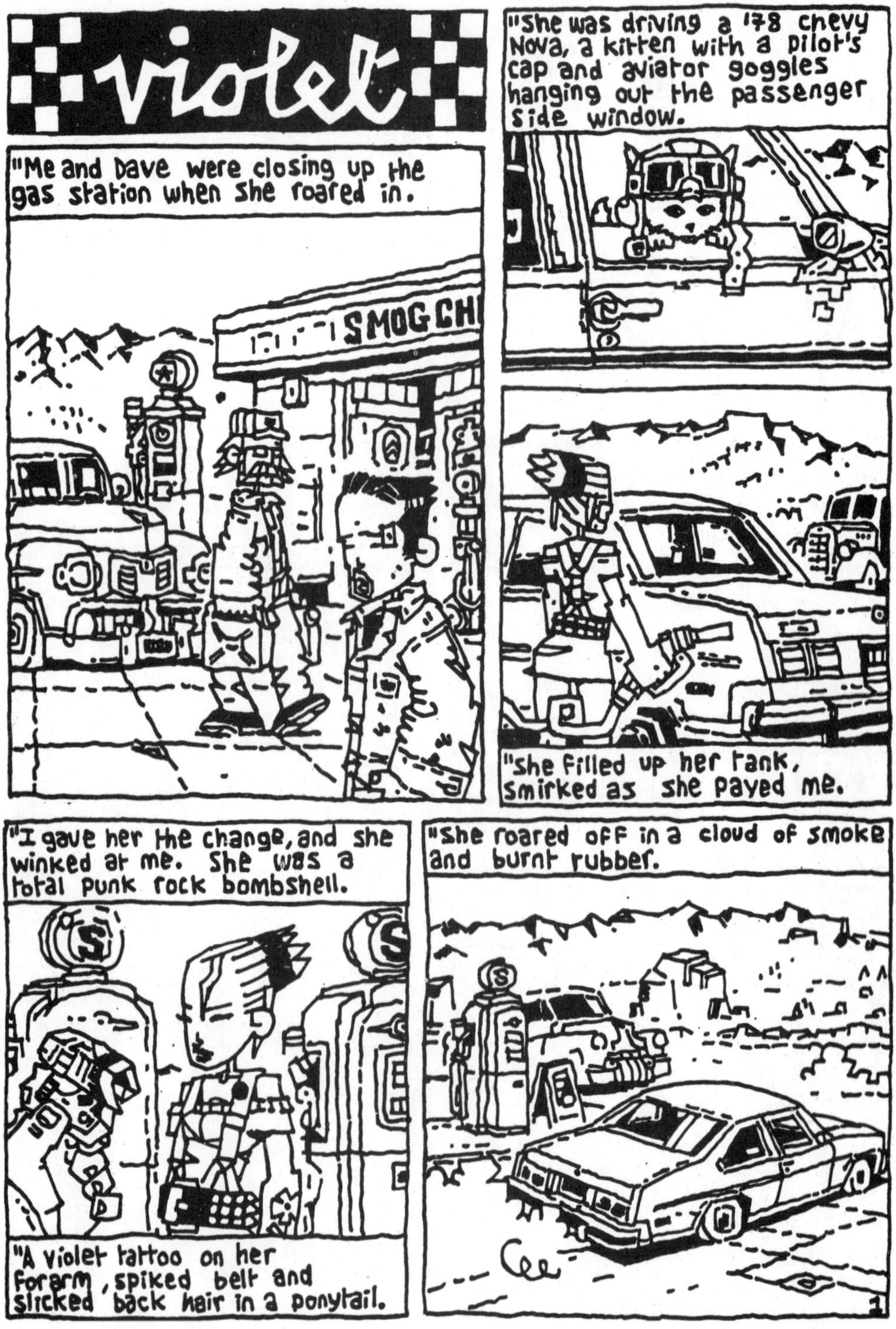
violet
"Me and Dave were closing up the gas station when she roared in.
SMOG CH
"She was driving a '78 chevy Nova, a kitten with a pilot's cap and aviator goggles hanging out the passenger side window.
"She filled up her tank, smirked as she payed me.
"I gave her the change, and she winked at me. She was a total punk rock bombshell.
"A violet tattoo on her forarm, spiked belt and slicked back hair in a ponytail.
"She roared off in a cloud of smoke and burnt rubber.
Cee

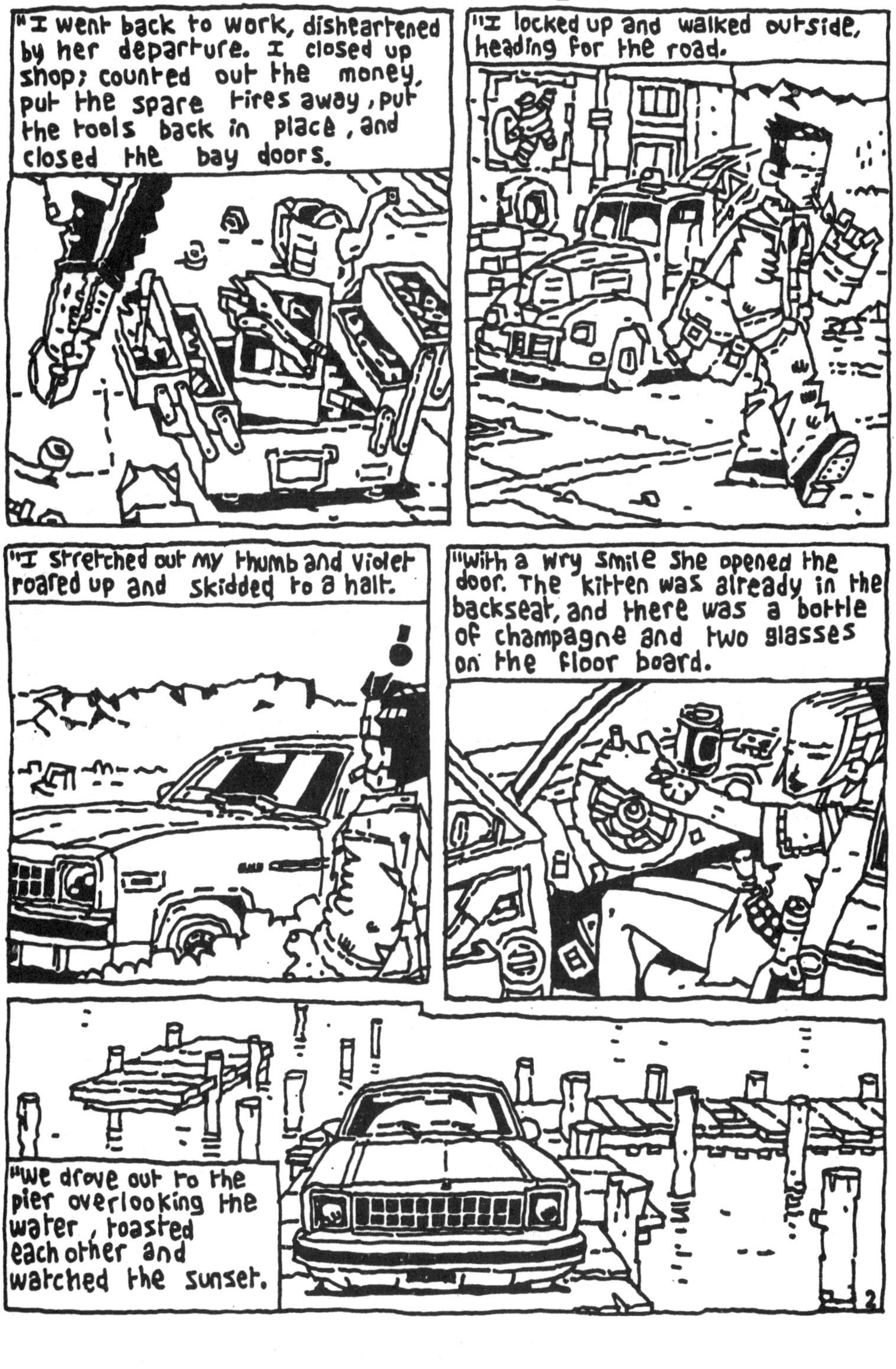
"I went back to work, disheartened by her departure. I closed up shop; counted out the money, put the spare tires away, put the tools back in place, and closed the bay doors.
"I locked up and walked outside, heading for the road.
"I stretched out my thumb and Violet roared up and skidded to a halt.
"With a wry smile she opened the door. The kitten was already in the backseat, and there was a bottle of champagne and two glasses on the floor board.
"We drove out to the pier overlooking the water, toasted each other and watched the sunset.

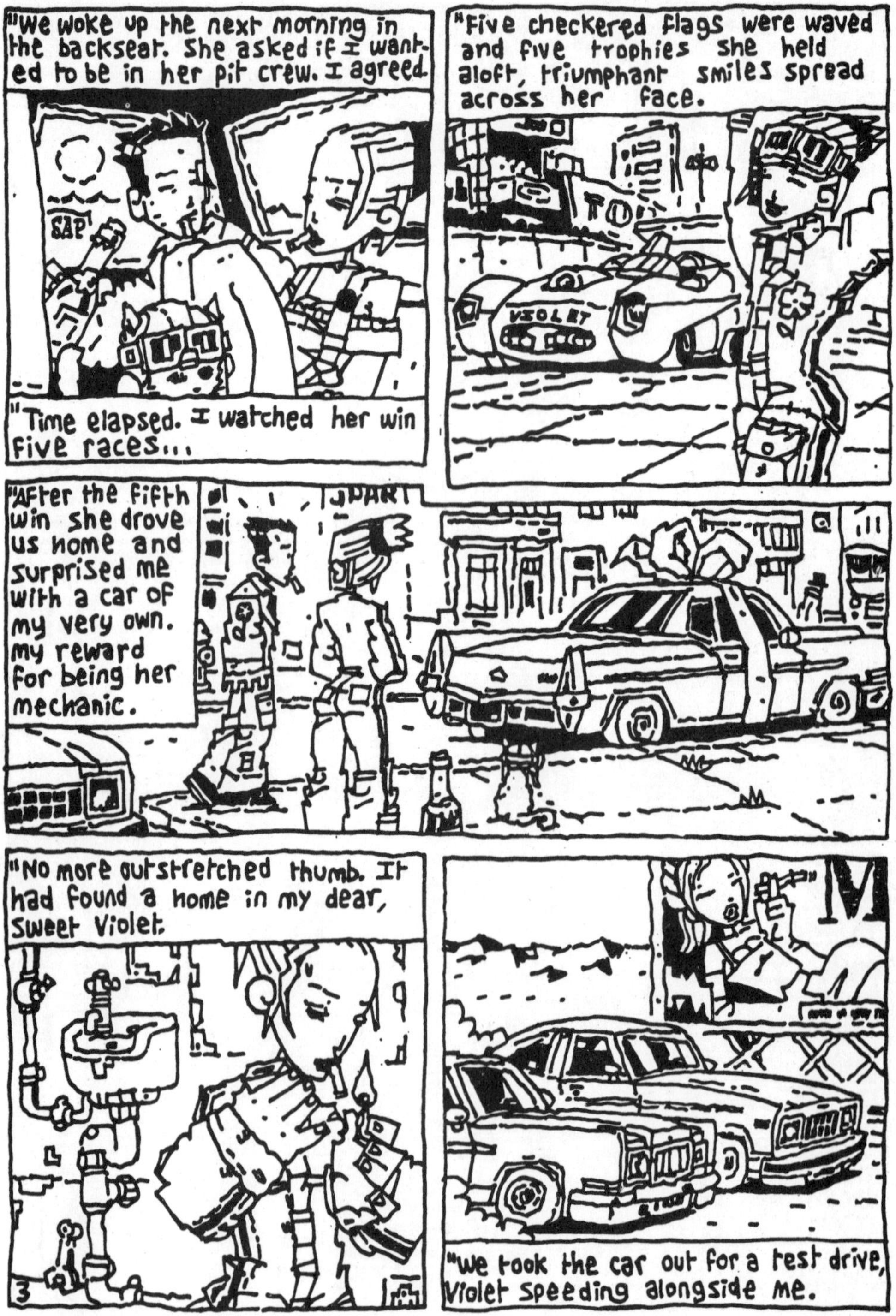
"We woke up the next morning in the backseat. She asked if I wanted to be in her pit crew. I agreed.
SAP
"Time elapsed. I watched her win five races...
"Five checkered flags were waved and five trophies she held aloft, triumphant smiles spread across her face.
VIOLET
"After the fifth win she drove us home and surprised me with a car of my very own. My reward for being her mechanic.
"No more outstretched thumb. It had found a home in my dear, sweet Violet.
3
"We took the car out for a test drive, Violet speeding alongside me.

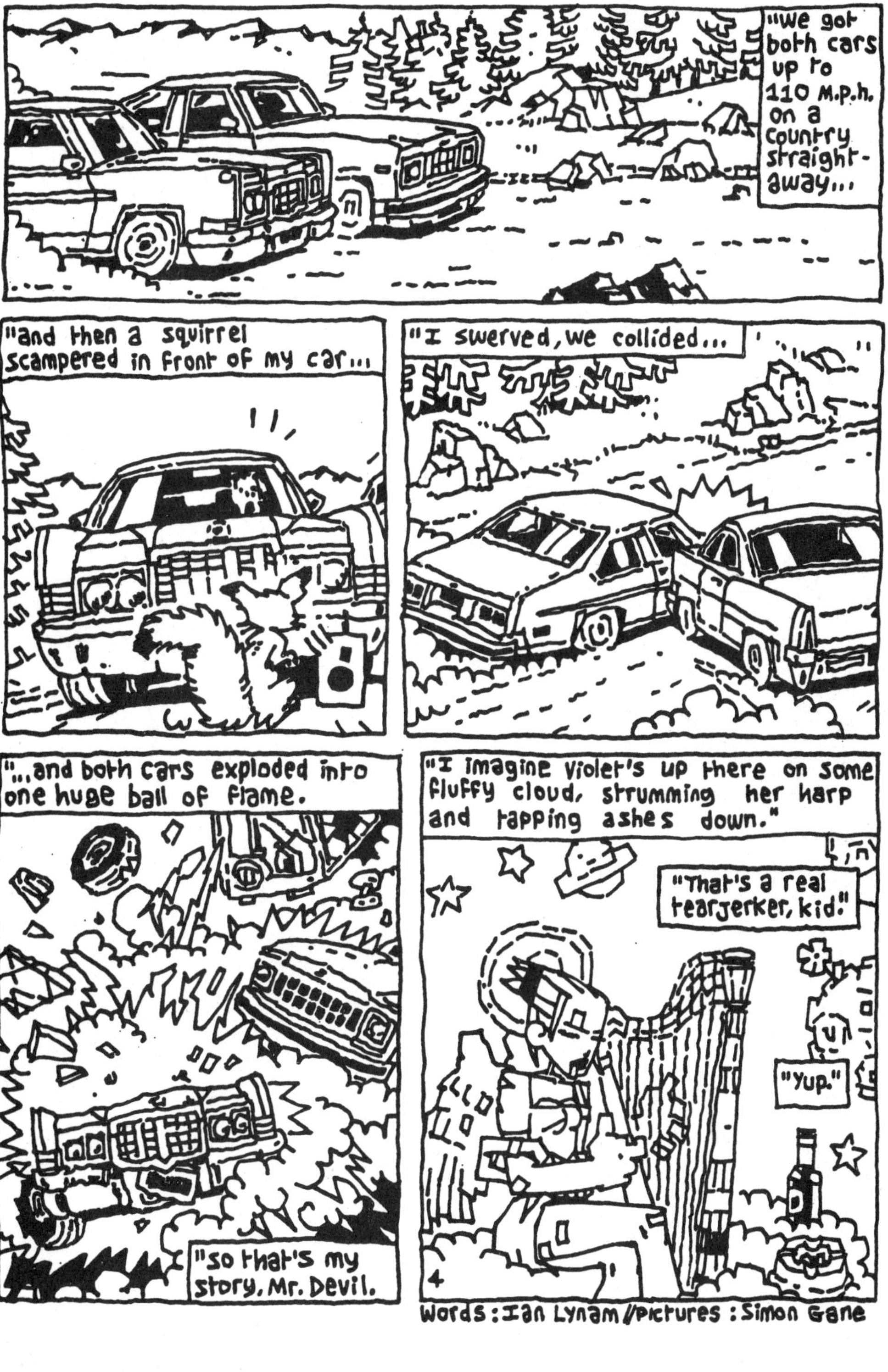
"we got both cars up to 110 M.p.h. on a country straight-away...
"and then a squirrel scampered in front of my car...
"I swerved, we collided...
"...and both cars exploded into one huge ball of flame.
"so that's my story, Mr. Devil.
"I imagine violet's up there on some fluffy cloud, strumming her harp and tapping ashes down."
"That's a real tearjerker, kid."
"Yup."
4
Words : Ian Lynam // Pictures : Simon Gane

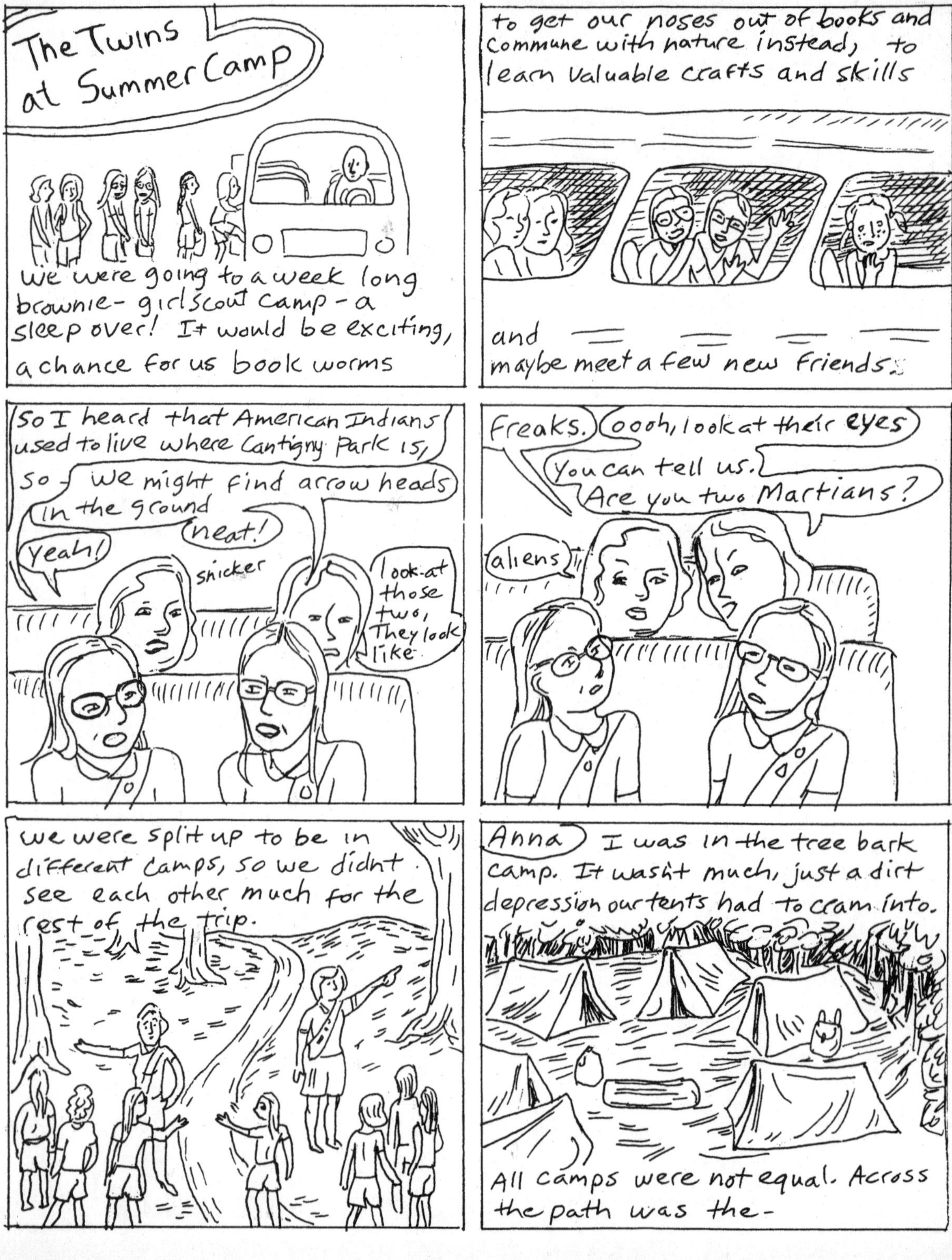
The Twins at Summer Camp
We were going to a week long brownie- girlscout camp - a sleep over! It would be exciting, a chance for us book worms
to get our noses out of books and commune with nature instead, to learn valuable crafts and skills
and maybe meet a few new friends...
So I heard that American Indians used to live where Cantigny Park is,
so - we might find arrow heads in the ground
Yeah!
neat!
snicker
look at those two, They look like
Freaks.
oooh, look at their eyes
You can tell us.
Are you two Martians?
aliens
We were split up to be in different camps, so we didnt see each other much for the rest of the trip.
Anna
I was in the tree bark camp. It wasn't much, just a dirt depression our tents had to cram into.
All camps were not equal. Across the path was the-

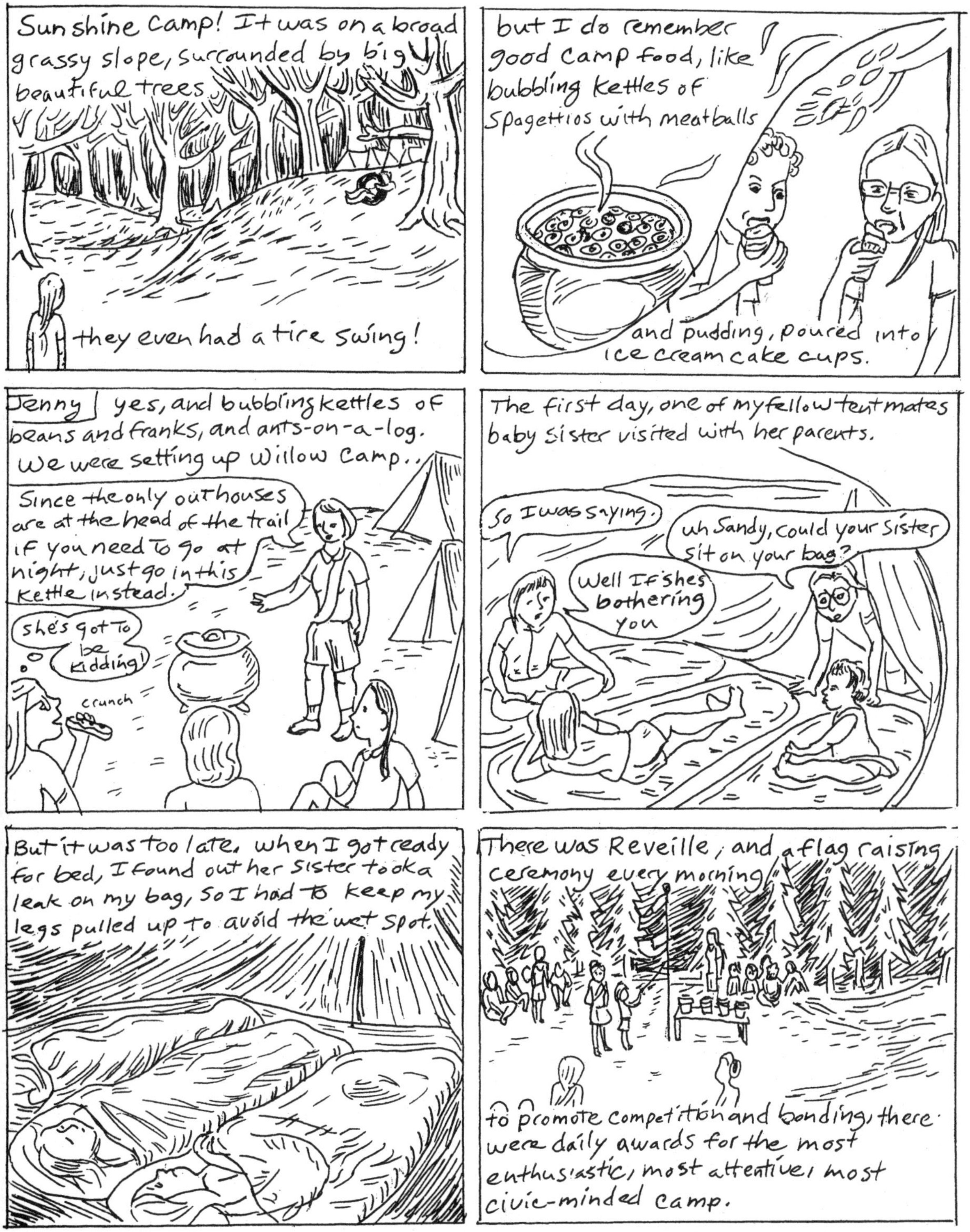
Sunshine Camp! It was on a broad grassy slope, surrounded by big beautiful trees
they even had a tire swing!
but I do remember good camp food, like bubbling kettles of Spagettios with meatballs
and pudding, poured into ice cream cake cups.
Jenny
yes, and bubbling kettles of beans and franks, and ants-on-a-log. We were setting up Willow Camp..
Since the only outhouses are at the head of the trail if you need to go at night, just go in this kettle instead.
she's got to be kidding!
crunch
The first day, one of my fellow tent mates baby sister visited with her parents.
So I was saying.
uh Sandy, could your sister sit on your bag?
Well If she's bothering you
But it was too late. when I got ready for bed, I found out her sister took a leak on my bag, so I had to keep my legs pulled up to avoid the wet spot.
There was Reveille, and a flag raising ceremony every morning
to promote competition and bonding, there were daily awards for the most enthusiastic, most attentive, most civic-minded camp.

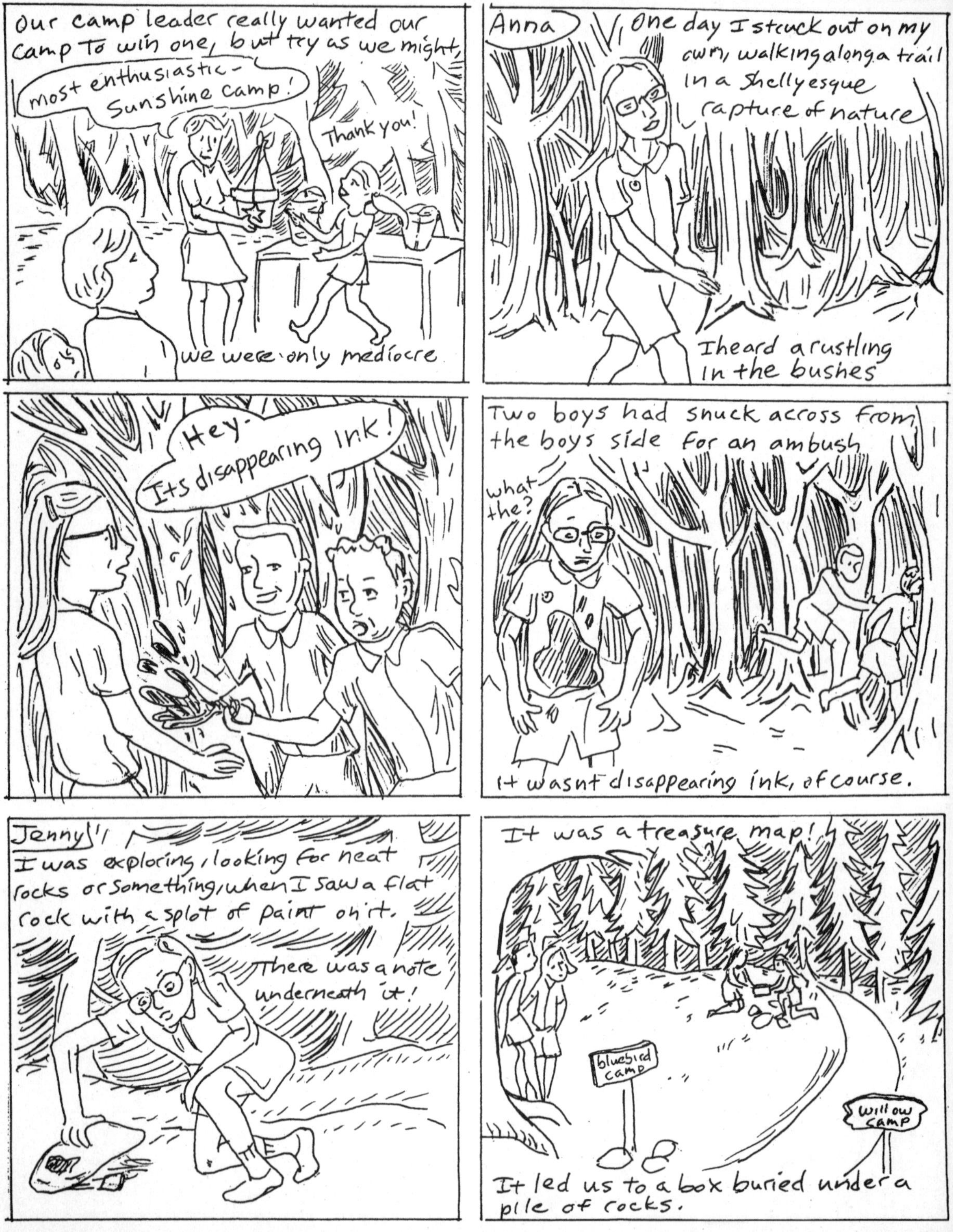
Our camp leader really wanted our camp to win one, but try as we might,
most enthusiastic - Sunshine camp!
Thank you!
we were only mediocre
Anna
One day I struck out on my own, walking along a trail in a Shellyesque rapture of nature
I heard a rustling in the bushes
Hey - It's disappearing ink!
Two boys had snuck across from the boys side for an ambush
what the?
It wasnt disappearing ink, of course.
Jenny
I was exploring, looking for neat rocks or something, when I saw a flat rock with a splot of paint on it.
There was a note underneath it!
It was a treasure map!
bluebird camp
willow camp
It led us to a box buried under a pile of rocks.

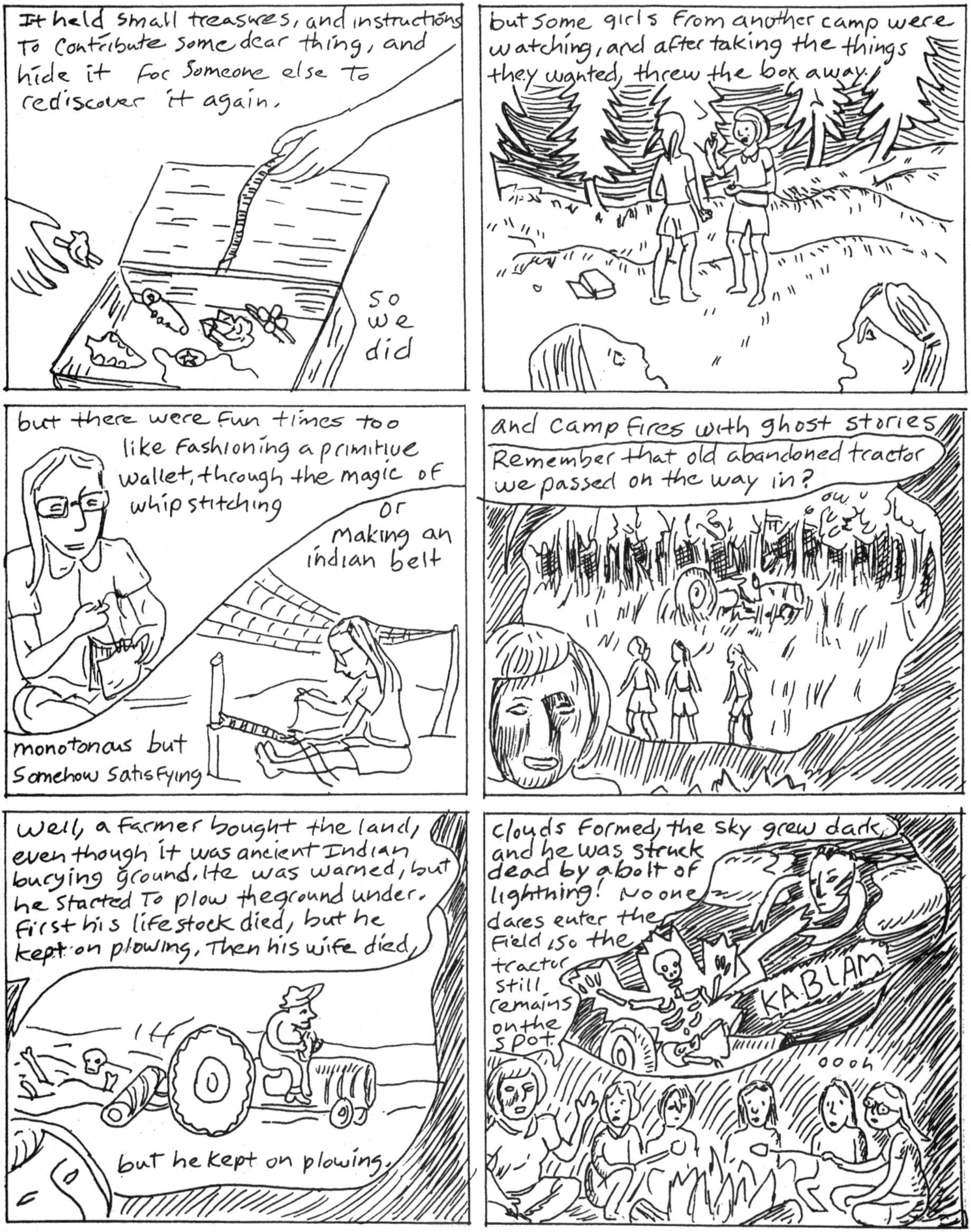
It held small treasures, and instructions to contribute some dear thing, and hide it for someone else to rediscover it again.
so we did
but some girls from another camp were watching, and after taking the things they wanted, threw the box away.
but there were fun times too
like fashioning a primitive wallet, through the magic of whipstitching
or making an indian belt
monotonous but somehow satisfying
and camp fires with ghost stories
Remember that old abandoned tractor we passed on the way in?
Well, a farmer bought the land, even though it was ancient Indian burying ground. He was warned, but he started to plow the ground under. First his lifestock died, but he kept on plowing. Then his wife died,
but he kept on plowing.
clouds formed, the sky grew dark, and he was struck dead by a bolt of lightning! No one dares enter the field, so the tractor still remains on the spot.
KABLAM
oooh

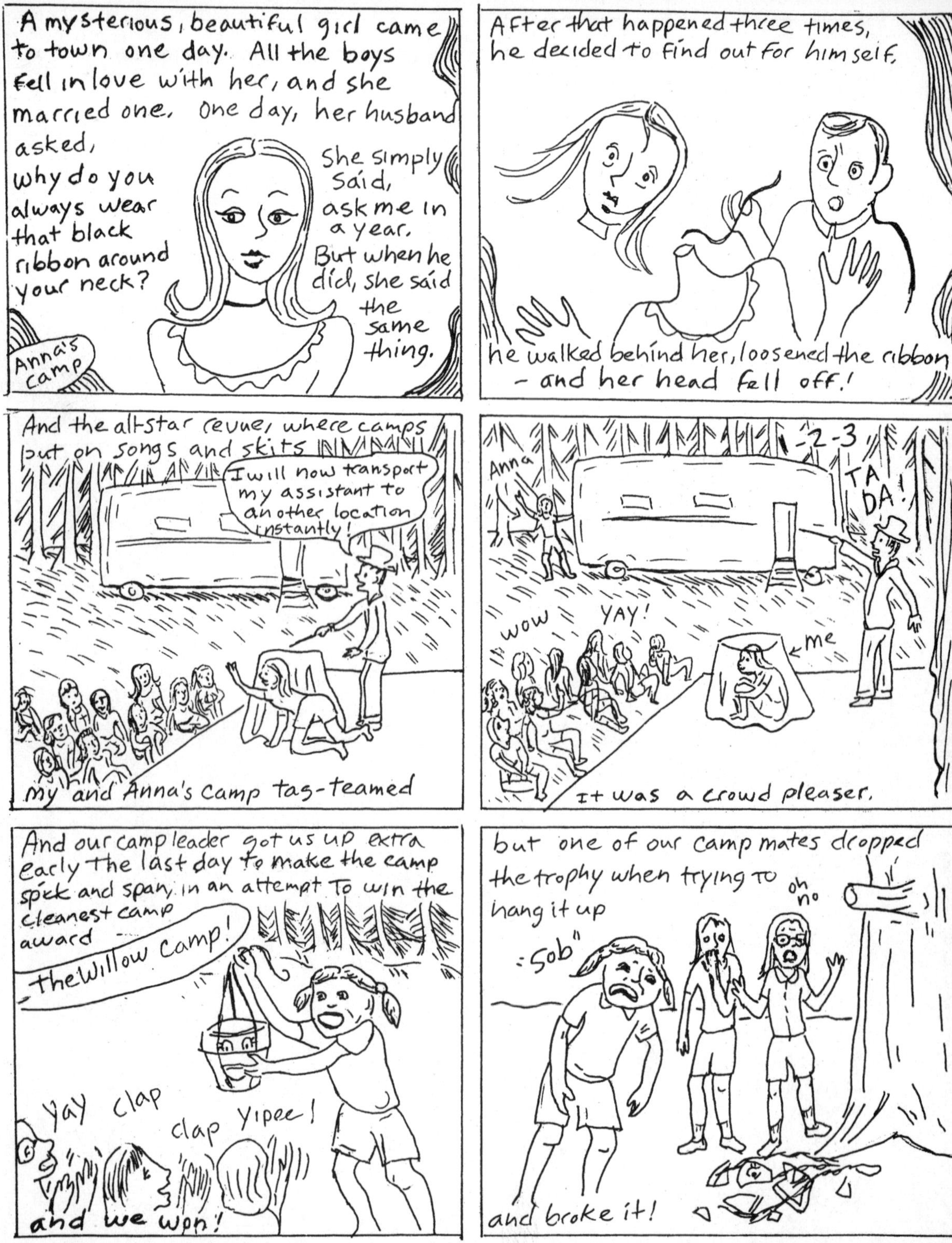

A mysterious, beautiful girl came to town one day. All the boys fell in love with her, and she married one. One day, her husband asked,
why do you always wear that black ribbon around your neck?
She simply said, ask me in a year. But when he did, she said the same thing.
Anna's camp
After that happened three times, he decided to find out for himself.
he walked behind her, loosened the ribbon - and her head fell off!
And the all-star revue, where camps put on songs and skits
I will now transport my assistant to another location instantly!
my and Anna's camp tag-teamed
Anna
1-2-3
TA DA!
wow
YAY!
me
It was a crowd pleaser.
And our camp leader got us up extra early the last day to make the camp spick and span in an attempt to win the cleanest camp award
the Willow camp!
yay clap
clap yipee!
and we won!
but one of our camp mates dropped the trophy when trying to hang it up
oh no
"sob"
and broke it!

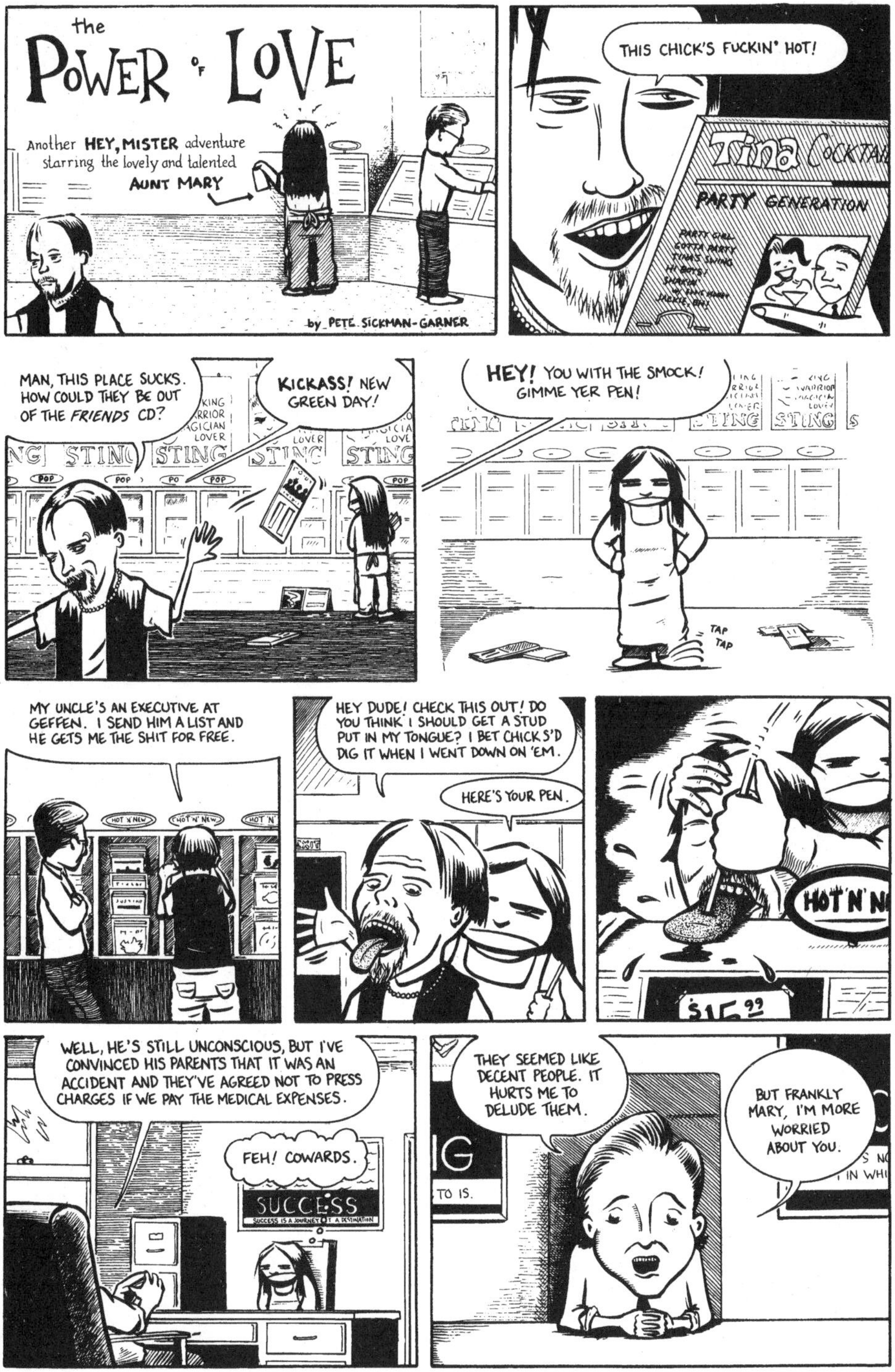
the POWER of LOVE
Another HEY, MISTER adventure starring the lovely and talented AUNT MARY
by PETE SICKMAN-GARNER
THIS CHICK'S FUCKIN' HOT!
Tina COCKTAIL
PARTY GENERATION
MAN, THIS PLACE SUCKS. HOW COULD THEY BE OUT OF THE FRIENDS CD?
KICKASS! NEW GREEN DAY!
STING
POP
HEY! YOU WITH THE SMOCK! GIMME YER PEN!
TAP TAP
MY UNCLE'S AN EXECUTIVE AT GEFFEN. I SEND HIM A LIST AND HE GETS ME THE SHIT FOR FREE.
HOT 'N' NEW
HEY DUDE! CHECK THIS OUT! DO YOU THINK I SHOULD GET A STUD PUT IN MY TONGUE? I BET CHICKS'D DIG IT WHEN I WENT DOWN ON 'EM.
HERE'S YOUR PEN.
HOT 'N' N
WELL, HE'S STILL UNCONSCIOUS, BUT I'VE CONVINCED HIS PARENTS THAT IT WAS AN ACCIDENT AND THEY'VE AGREED NOT TO PRESS CHARGES IF WE PAY THE MEDICAL EXPENSES.
FEH! COWARDS.
SUCCESS
THEY SEEMED LIKE DECENT PEOPLE. IT HURTS ME TO DELUDE THEM.
BUT FRANKLY MARY, I'M MORE WORRIED ABOUT YOU.

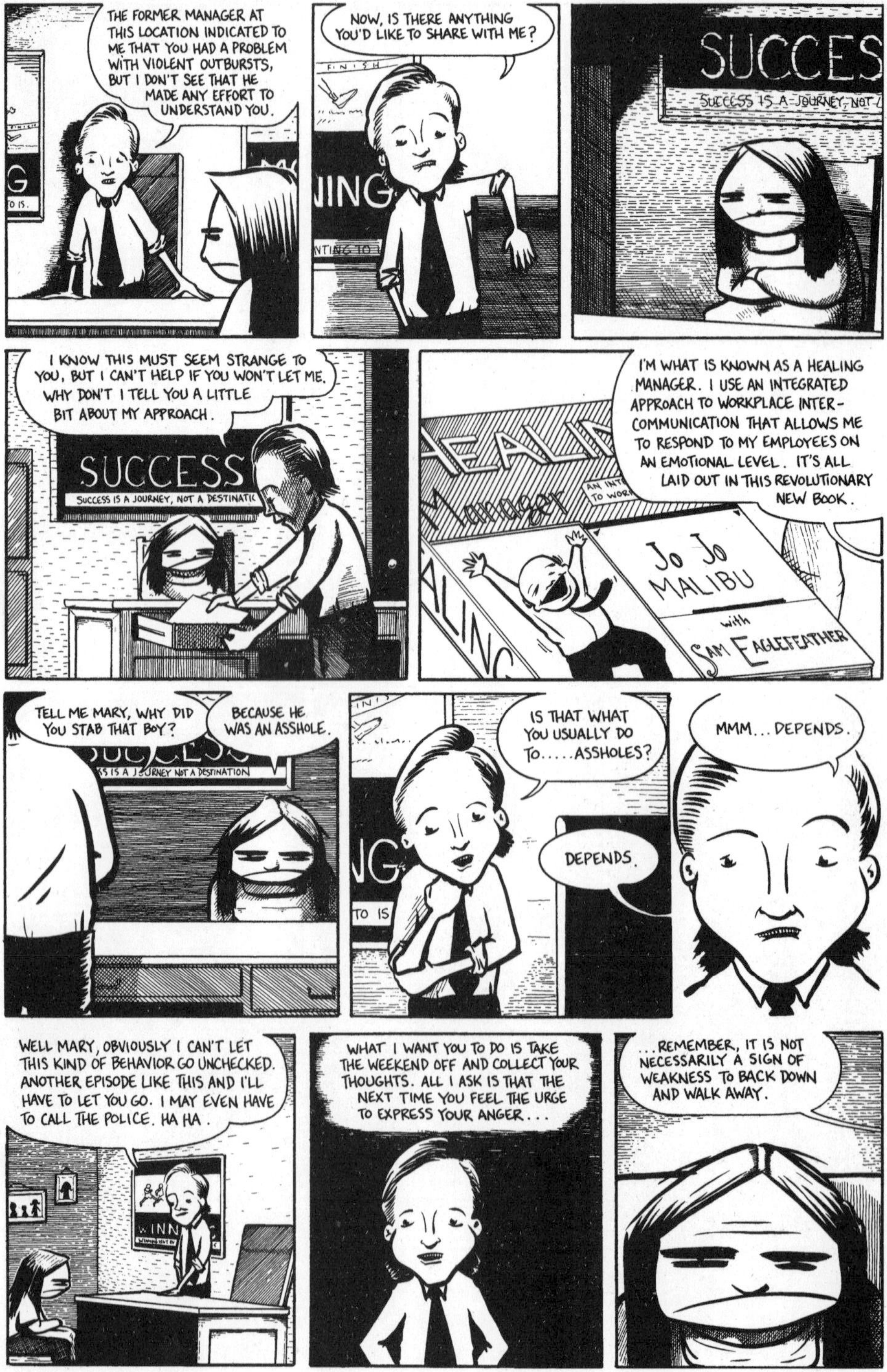
THE FORMER MANAGER AT THIS LOCATION INDICATED TO ME THAT YOU HAD A PROBLEM WITH VIOLENT OUTBURSTS, BUT I DON'T SEE THAT HE MADE ANY EFFORT TO UNDERSTAND YOU.
NOW, IS THERE ANYTHING YOU'D LIKE TO SHARE WITH ME?
SUCCES
SUCCESS IS A JOURNEY, NOT
I KNOW THIS MUST SEEM STRANGE TO YOU, BUT I CAN'T HELP IF YOU WON'T LET ME. WHY DON'T I TELL YOU A LITTLE BIT ABOUT MY APPROACH.
SUCCESS
SUCCESS IS A JOURNEY, NOT A DESTINATIC
I'M WHAT IS KNOWN AS A HEALING MANAGER. I USE AN INTEGRATED APPROACH TO WORKPLACE INTER-COMMUNICATION THAT ALLOWS ME TO RESPOND TO MY EMPLOYEES ON AN EMOTIONAL LEVEL. IT'S ALL LAID OUT IN THIS REVOLUTIONARY NEW BOOK.
Manager
Jo Jo MALIBU
with
SAM EAGLEFEATHER
TELL ME MARY, WHY DID YOU STAB THAT BOY?
BECAUSE HE WAS AN ASSHOLE.
IS THAT WHAT YOU USUALLY DO TO..... ASSHOLES?
DEPENDS.
MMM... DEPENDS.
WELL MARY, OBVIOUSLY I CAN'T LET THIS KIND OF BEHAVIOR GO UNCHECKED. ANOTHER EPISODE LIKE THIS AND I'LL HAVE TO LET YOU GO. I MAY EVEN HAVE TO CALL THE POLICE. HA HA.
WHAT I WANT YOU TO DO IS TAKE THE WEEKEND OFF AND COLLECT YOUR THOUGHTS. ALL I ASK IS THAT THE NEXT TIME YOU FEEL THE URGE TO EXPRESS YOUR ANGER...
...REMEMBER, IT IS NOT NECESSARILY A SIGN OF WEAKNESS TO BACK DOWN AND WALK AWAY.

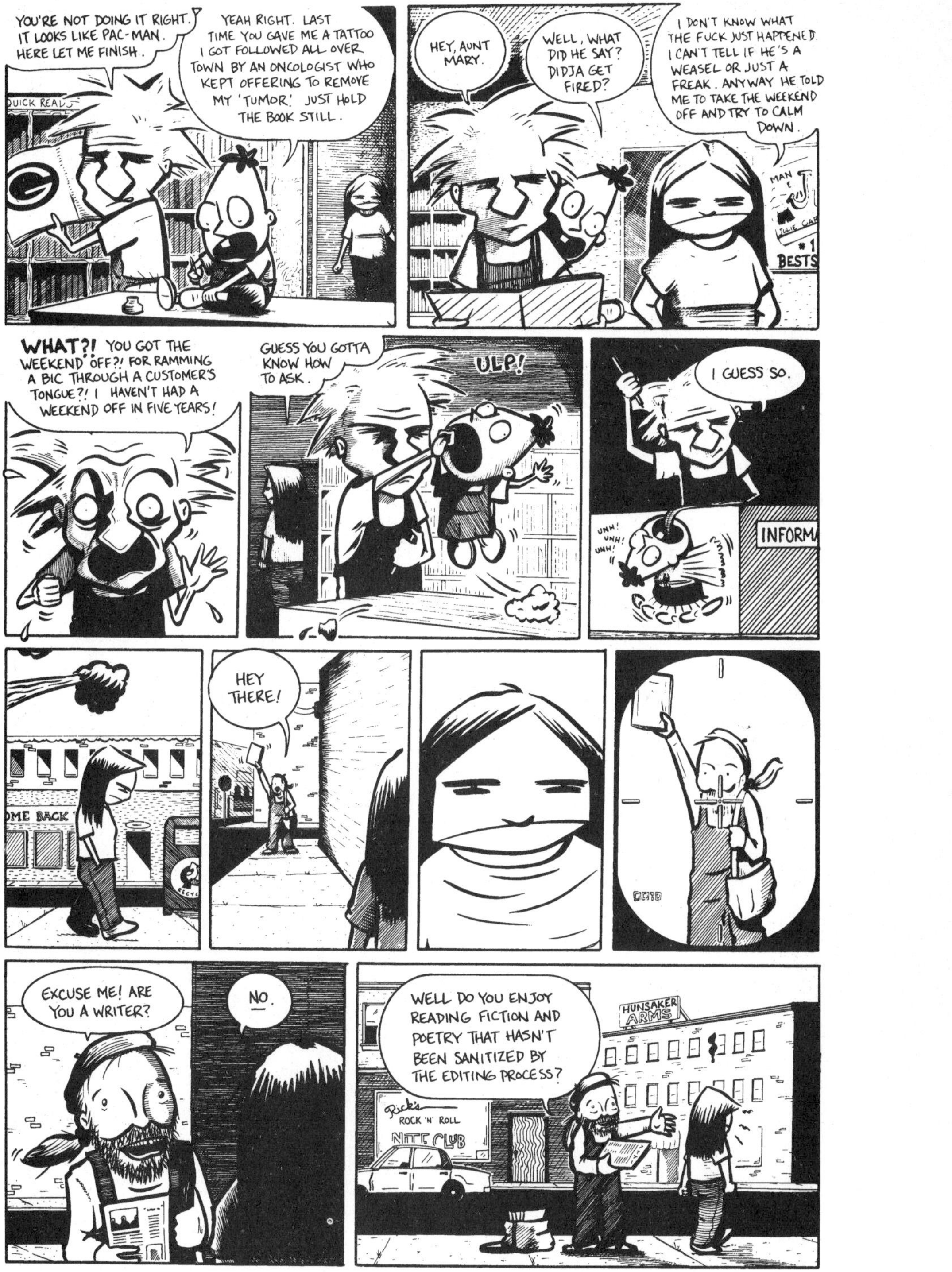

YOU'RE NOT DOING IT RIGHT. IT LOOKS LIKE PAC-MAN. HERE LET ME FINISH.
YEAH RIGHT. LAST TIME YOU GAVE ME A TATTOO I GOT FOLLOWED ALL OVER TOWN BY AN ONCOLOGIST WHO KEPT OFFERING TO REMOVE MY 'TUMOR.' JUST HOLD THE BOOK STILL.
QUICK READS
HEY, AUNT MARY.
WELL, WHAT DID HE SAY? DIDJA GET FIRED?
I DON'T KNOW WHAT THE FUCK JUST HAPPENED. I CAN'T TELL IF HE'S A WEASEL OR JUST A FREAK. ANYWAY HE TOLD ME TO TAKE THE WEEKEND OFF AND TRY TO CALM DOWN.
WHAT?! YOU GOT THE WEEKEND OFF?! FOR RAMMING A BIC THROUGH A CUSTOMER'S TONGUE?! I HAVEN'T HAD A WEEKEND OFF IN FIVE YEARS!
GUESS YOU GOTTA KNOW HOW TO ASK.
ULP!
I GUESS SO.
UNH! UNH! UNH!
INFORMA
HEY THERE!
EXCUSE ME! ARE YOU A WRITER?
NO.
WELL DO YOU ENJOY READING FICTION AND POETRY THAT HASN'T BEEN SANITIZED BY THE EDITING PROCESS?
HUNSAKER ARMS
Rick's ROCK 'N' ROLL NITE CLUB

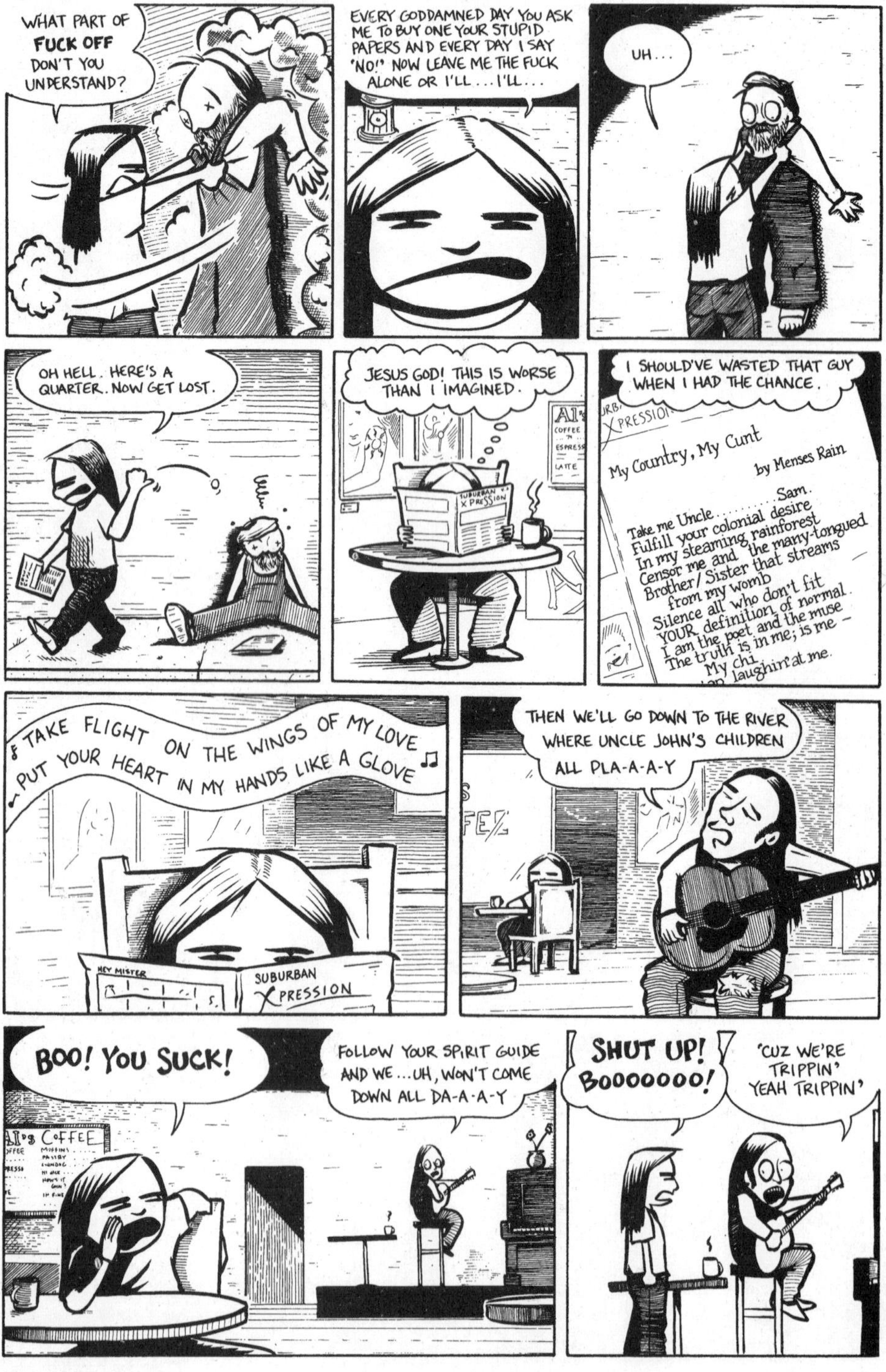
WHAT PART OF FUCK OFF DON'T YOU UNDERSTAND?
EVERY GODDAMNED DAY YOU ASK ME TO BUY ONE YOUR STUPID PAPERS AND EVERY DAY I SAY 'NO!' NOW LEAVE ME THE FUCK ALONE OR I'LL... I'LL...
UH...
OH HELL. HERE'S A QUARTER. NOW GET LOST.
JESUS GOD! THIS IS WORSE THAN I IMAGINED.
SUBURBAN XPRESSION
AL's COFFEE ESPRESSO LATTE
I SHOULD'VE WASTED THAT GUY WHEN I HAD THE CHANCE.
My Country, My Cunt
by Menses Rain
Take me Uncle..........Sam.
Fulfill your colonial desire
In my steaming rainforest
Censor me and the many-tongued
Brother/Sister that streams
from my womb
Silence all who don't fit
YOUR definition of normal.
I am the poet and the muse
The truth is in me; is me —
My chi
laughin' at me.
TAKE FLIGHT ON THE WINGS OF MY LOVE
PUT YOUR HEART IN MY HANDS LIKE A GLOVE
HEY MISTER
SUBURBAN XPRESSION
THEN WE'LL GO DOWN TO THE RIVER WHERE UNCLE JOHN'S CHILDREN ALL PLA-A-A-Y
BOO! YOU SUCK!
FOLLOW YOUR SPIRIT GUIDE AND WE... UH, WON'T COME DOWN ALL DA-A-A-Y
AL's COFFEE
SHUT UP! BOOOOOOO!
'CUZ WE'RE TRIPPIN' YEAH TRIPPIN'

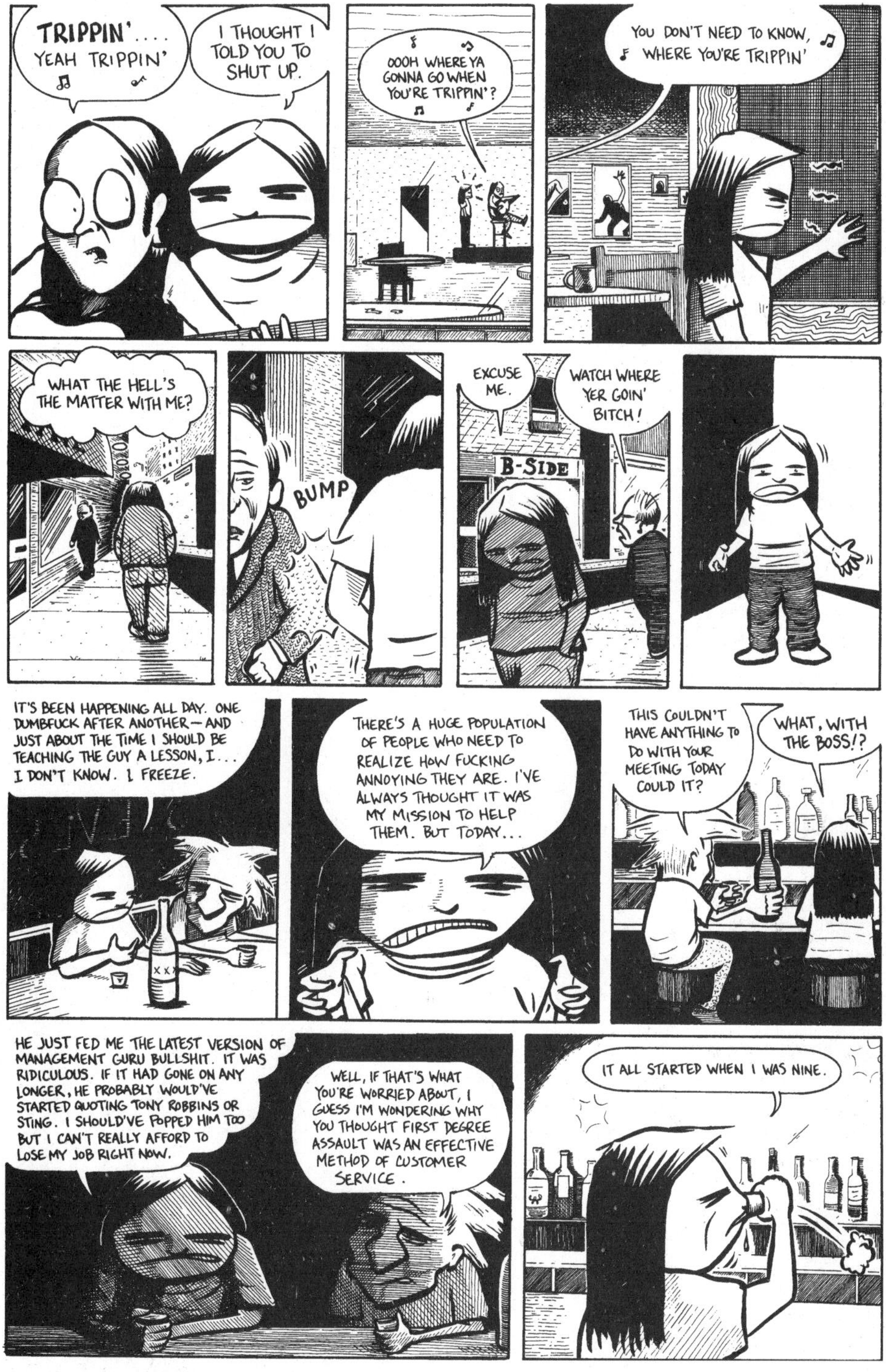
TRIPPIN'.... YEAH TRIPPIN'
I THOUGHT I TOLD YOU TO SHUT UP.
OOOH WHERE YA GONNA GO WHEN YOU'RE TRIPPIN'?
YOU DON'T NEED TO KNOW, WHERE YOU'RE TRIPPIN'
WHAT THE HELL'S THE MATTER WITH ME?
BUMP
EXCUSE ME.
WATCH WHERE YER GOIN' BITCH!
B-SIDE
IT'S BEEN HAPPENING ALL DAY. ONE DUMBFUCK AFTER ANOTHER— AND JUST ABOUT THE TIME I SHOULD BE TEACHING THE GUY A LESSON, I... I DON'T KNOW. I FREEZE.
THERE'S A HUGE POPULATION OF PEOPLE WHO NEED TO REALIZE HOW FUCKING ANNOYING THEY ARE. I'VE ALWAYS THOUGHT IT WAS MY MISSION TO HELP THEM. BUT TODAY...
THIS COULDN'T HAVE ANYTHING TO DO WITH YOUR MEETING TODAY COULD IT?
WHAT, WITH THE BOSS!?
HE JUST FED ME THE LATEST VERSION OF MANAGEMENT GURU BULLSHIT. IT WAS RIDICULOUS. IF IT HAD GONE ON ANY LONGER, HE PROBABLY WOULD'VE STARTED QUOTING TONY ROBBINS OR STING. I SHOULD'VE POPPED HIM TOO BUT I CAN'T REALLY AFFORD TO LOSE MY JOB RIGHT NOW.
WELL, IF THAT'S WHAT YOU'RE WORRIED ABOUT, I GUESS I'M WONDERING WHY YOU THOUGHT FIRST DEGREE ASSAULT WAS AN EFFECTIVE METHOD OF CUSTOMER SERVICE.
IT ALL STARTED WHEN I WAS NINE.

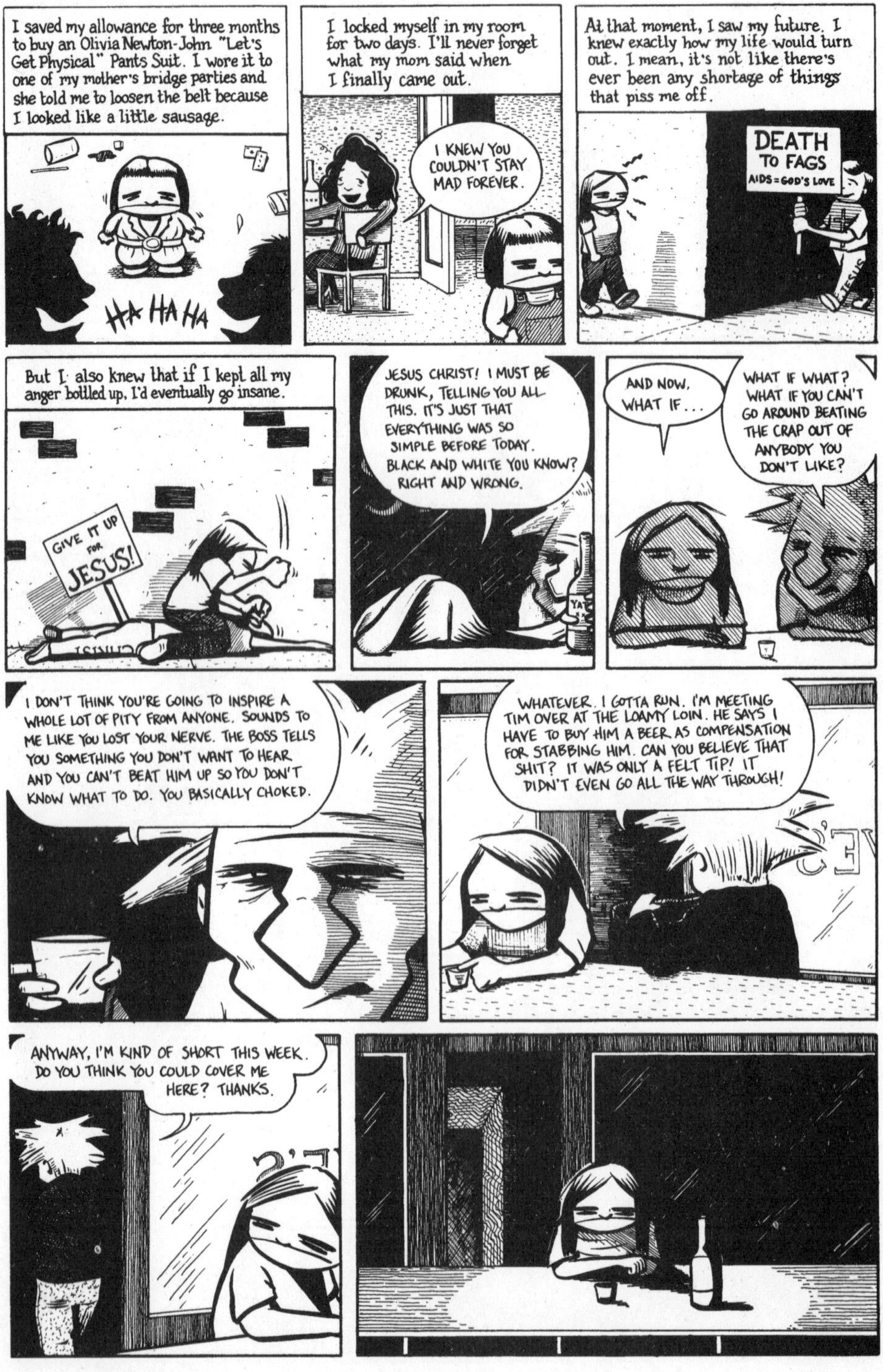
I saved my allowance for three months to buy an Olivia Newton-John "Let's Get Physical" Pants Suit. I wore it to one of my mother's bridge parties and she told me to loosen the belt because I looked like a little sausage.
HA HA HA
I locked myself in my room for two days. I'll never forget what my mom said when I finally came out.
I KNEW YOU COULDN'T STAY MAD FOREVER.
At that moment, I saw my future. I knew exactly how my life would turn out. I mean, it's not like there's ever been any shortage of things that piss me off.
DEATH TO FAGS
AIDS = GOD'S LOVE
JESUS
But I also knew that if I kept all my anger bottled up, I'd eventually go insane.
GIVE IT UP FOR JESUS!
JESUS CHRIST! I MUST BE DRUNK, TELLING YOU ALL THIS. IT'S JUST THAT EVERYTHING WAS SO SIMPLE BEFORE TODAY. BLACK AND WHITE YOU KNOW? RIGHT AND WRONG.
AND NOW, WHAT IF...
WHAT IF WHAT? WHAT IF YOU CAN'T GO AROUND BEATING THE CRAP OUT OF ANYBODY YOU DON'T LIKE?
I DON'T THINK YOU'RE GOING TO INSPIRE A WHOLE LOT OF PITY FROM ANYONE. SOUNDS TO ME LIKE YOU LOST YOUR NERVE. THE BOSS TELLS YOU SOMETHING YOU DON'T WANT TO HEAR AND YOU CAN'T BEAT HIM UP SO YOU DON'T KNOW WHAT TO DO. YOU BASICALLY CHOKED.
WHATEVER. I GOTTA RUN. I'M MEETING TIM OVER AT THE LOAMY LOIN. HE SAYS I HAVE TO BUY HIM A BEER AS COMPENSATION FOR STABBING HIM. CAN YOU BELIEVE THAT SHIT? IT WAS ONLY A FELT TIP! IT DIDN'T EVEN GO ALL THE WAY THROUGH!
ANYWAY, I'M KIND OF SHORT THIS WEEK. DO YOU THINK YOU COULD COVER ME HERE? THANKS.

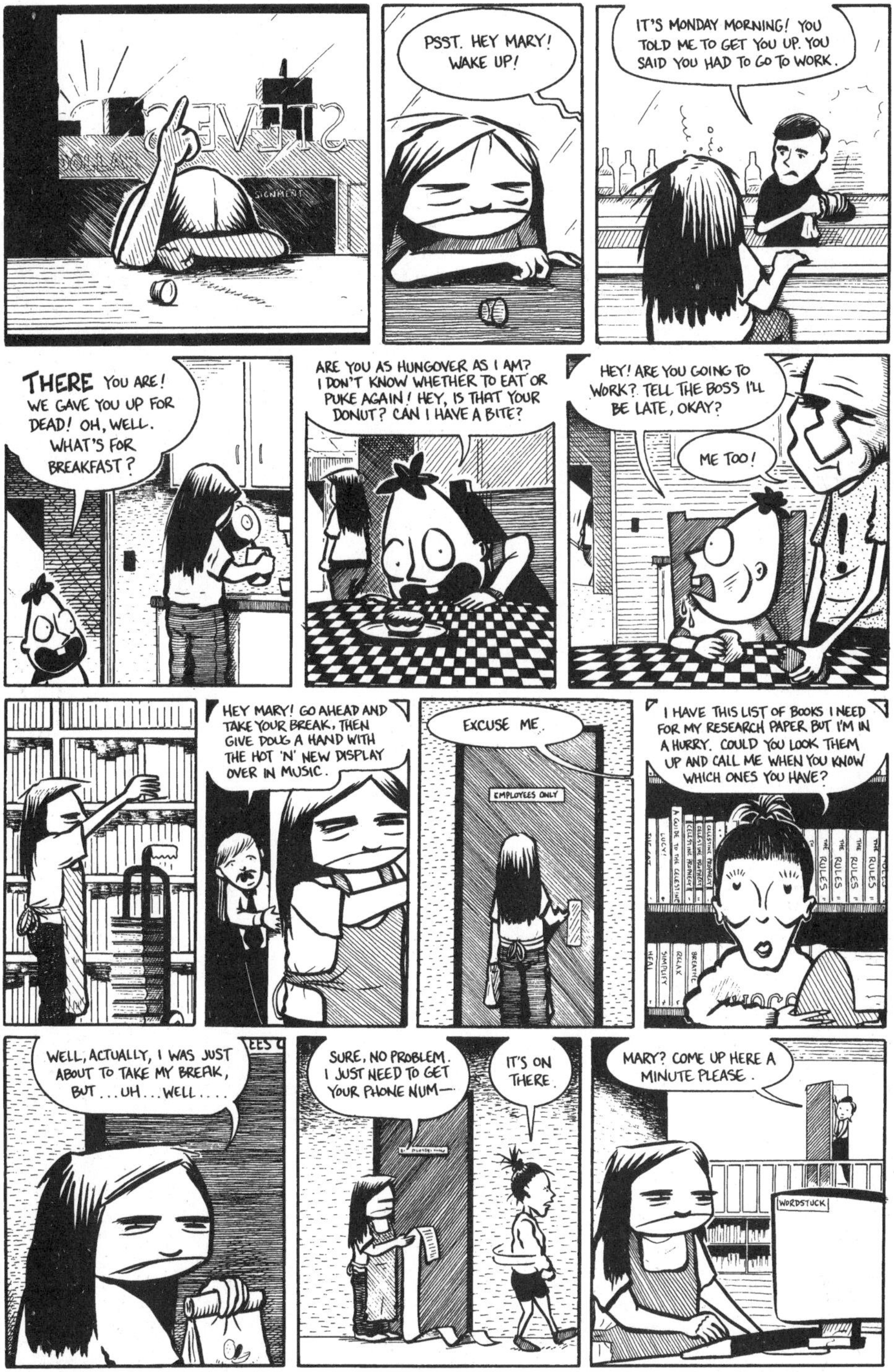
PSST. HEY MARY! WAKE UP!
IT'S MONDAY MORNING! YOU TOLD ME TO GET YOU UP. YOU SAID YOU HAD TO GO TO WORK.
THERE YOU ARE! WE GAVE YOU UP FOR DEAD! OH, WELL. WHAT'S FOR BREAKFAST?
ARE YOU AS HUNGOVER AS I AM? I DON'T KNOW WHETHER TO EAT OR PUKE AGAIN! HEY, IS THAT YOUR DONUT? CAN I HAVE A BITE?
HEY! ARE YOU GOING TO WORK? TELL THE BOSS I'LL BE LATE, OKAY?
ME TOO!
HEY MARY! GO AHEAD AND TAKE YOUR BREAK, THEN GIVE DOUG A HAND WITH THE HOT 'N' NEW DISPLAY OVER IN MUSIC.
EXCUSE ME.
EMPLOYEES ONLY
I HAVE THIS LIST OF BOOKS I NEED FOR MY RESEARCH PAPER BUT I'M IN A HURRY. COULD YOU LOOK THEM UP AND CALL ME WHEN YOU KNOW WHICH ONES YOU HAVE?
WELL, ACTUALLY, I WAS JUST ABOUT TO TAKE MY BREAK, BUT . . . UH . . . WELL . . . .
SURE, NO PROBLEM. I JUST NEED TO GET YOUR PHONE NUM—
IT'S ON THERE.
MARY? COME UP HERE A MINUTE PLEASE.
WORDSTUCK

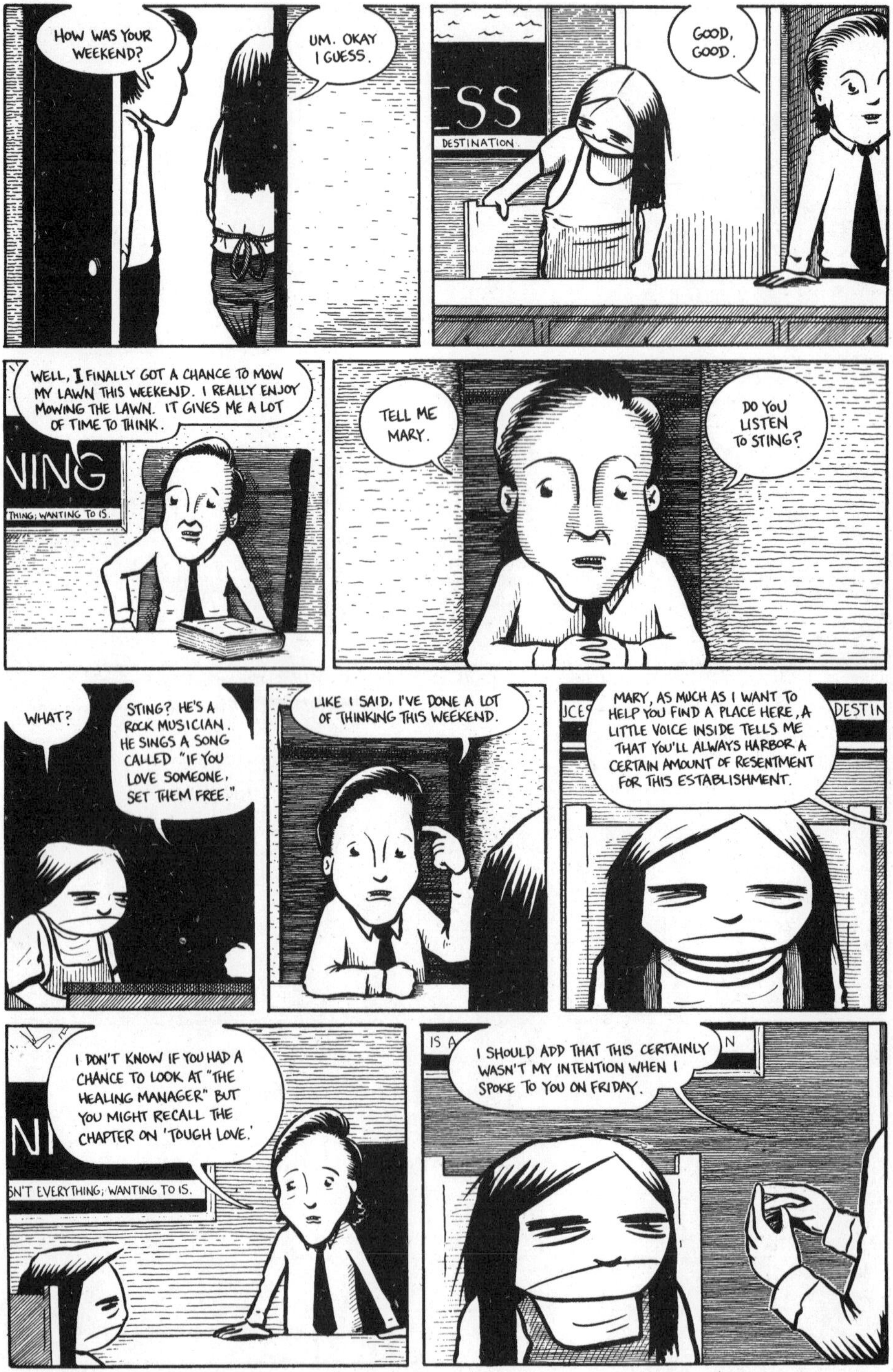
HOW WAS YOUR WEEKEND?
UM. OKAY I GUESS.
ESS
DESTINATION.
GOOD, GOOD.
WELL, I FINALLY GOT A CHANCE TO MOW MY LAWN THIS WEEKEND. I REALLY ENJOY MOWING THE LAWN. IT GIVES ME A LOT OF TIME TO THINK.
NING
THING; WANTING TO IS.
TELL ME MARY.
DO YOU LISTEN TO STING?
WHAT?
STING? HE'S A ROCK MUSICIAN. HE SINGS A SONG CALLED "IF YOU LOVE SOMEONE, SET THEM FREE."
LIKE I SAID, I'VE DONE A LOT OF THINKING THIS WEEKEND.
MARY, AS MUCH AS I WANT TO HELP YOU FIND A PLACE HERE, A LITTLE VOICE INSIDE TELLS ME THAT YOU'LL ALWAYS HARBOR A CERTAIN AMOUNT OF RESENTMENT FOR THIS ESTABLISHMENT.
DESTIN
I DON'T KNOW IF YOU HAD A CHANCE TO LOOK AT "THE HEALING MANAGER" BUT YOU MIGHT RECALL THE CHAPTER ON 'TOUGH LOVE.'
SN'T EVERYTHING; WANTING TO IS.
I SHOULD ADD THAT THIS CERTAINLY WASN'T MY INTENTION WHEN I SPOKE TO YOU ON FRIDAY.

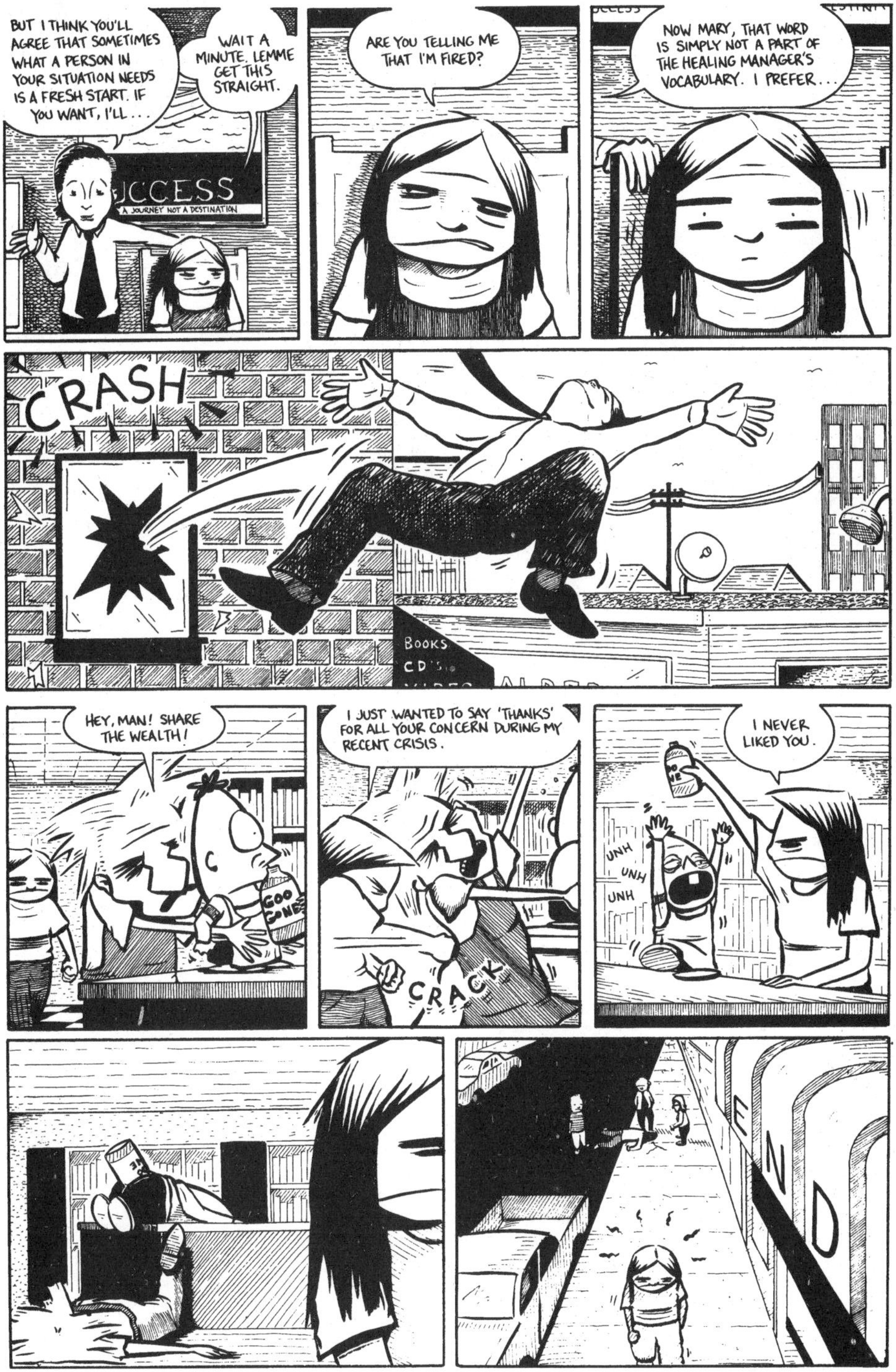
BUT I THINK YOU'LL AGREE THAT SOMETIMES WHAT A PERSON IN YOUR SITUATION NEEDS IS A FRESH START. IF YOU WANT, I'LL . . .
WAIT A MINUTE. LEMME GET THIS STRAIGHT.
UCCESS
A JOURNEY NOT A DESTINATION
ARE YOU TELLING ME THAT I'M FIRED?
NOW MARY, THAT WORD IS SIMPLY NOT A PART OF THE HEALING MANAGER'S VOCABULARY. I PREFER . . .
CRASH
BOOKS
CD'S
HEY, MAN! SHARE THE WEALTH!
GOO GONE
I JUST WANTED TO SAY 'THANKS' FOR ALL YOUR CONCERN DURING MY RECENT CRISIS.
CRACK
I NEVER LIKED YOU.
UNH
UNH
UNH
END

LAND OF

Westward, almost to the Pacific, in an ancient land settled by American only a century and a half ago.... A Volvo station wagon pulls up to the curb,

pulls over the curb and hits a metal sign post.... after a moment, the driver steps out of the car to inspect the damage. He has a shaved head,

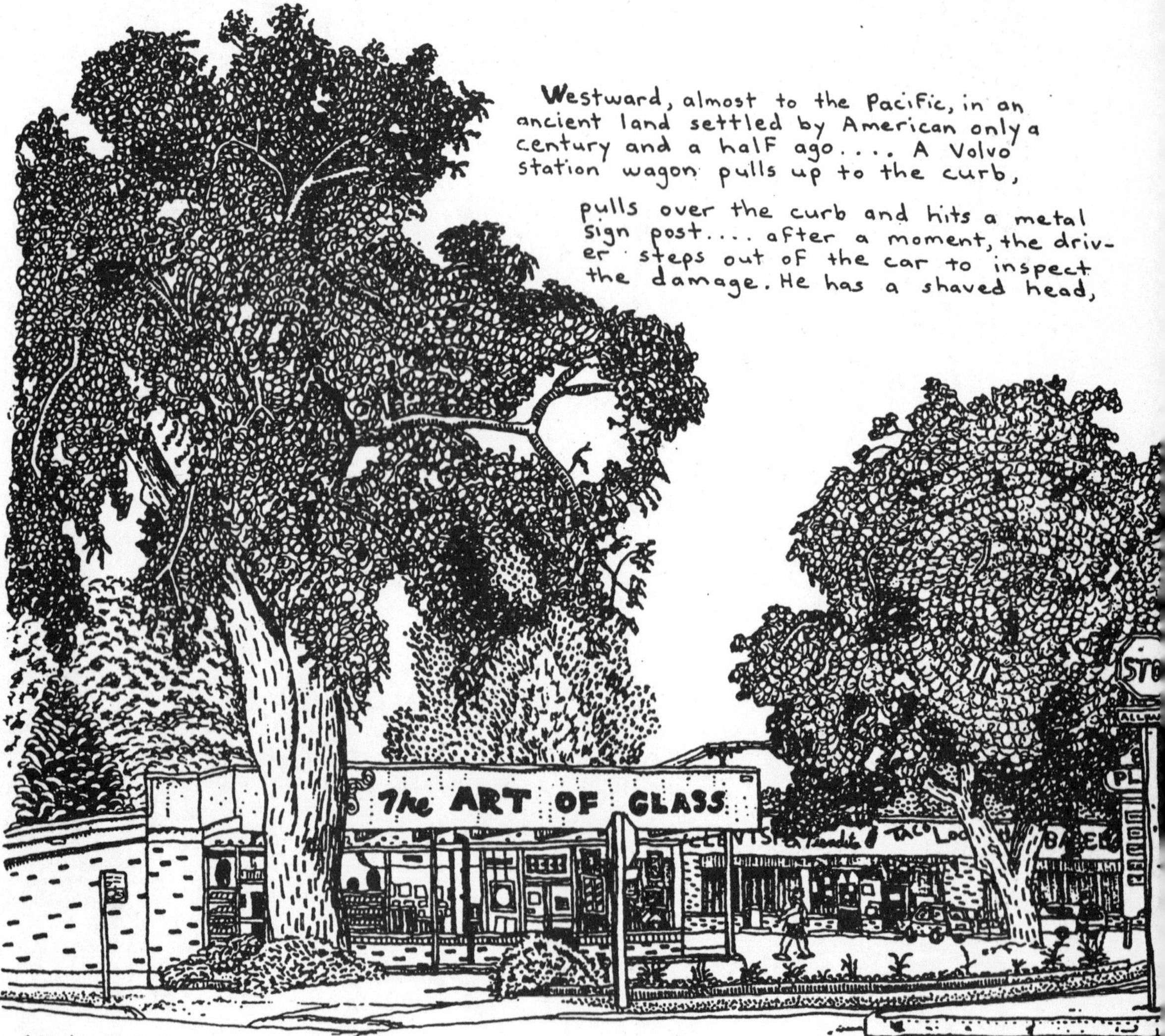

The ART OF GLASS
TACO

"Blair Street"
August '96
J. Zenick

PROMISE

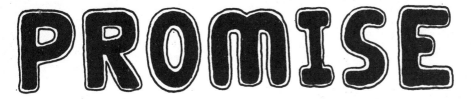

a worried look, and some sort of robe like a Hare Krisha or Kundalini Yoga practitioner.

Welcome to Eugene, where the holy don't quite have it together; where young women sit on bus benches waiting for the bus reading "Sailor's Song" by Ken Kesey; where one of

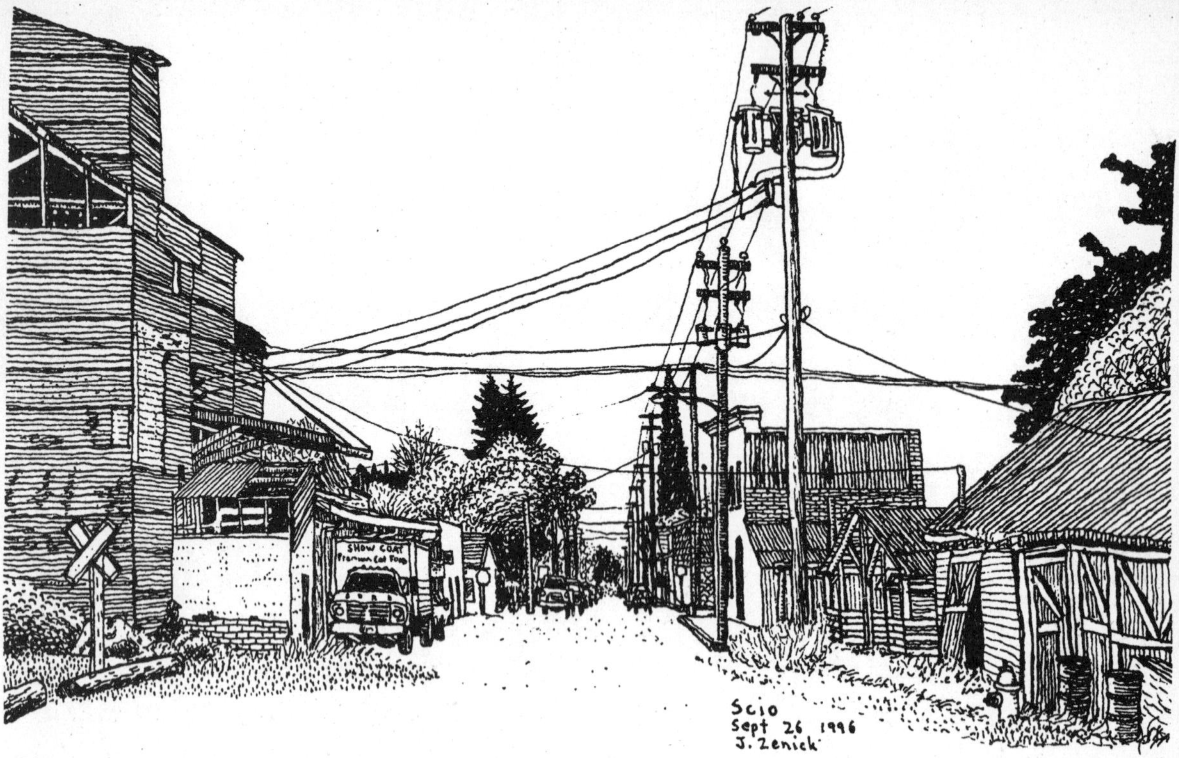
SNOW COAT
Premium Cat Food
Scio
Sept 26 1996
J. Zenick

Oregon's largest Universities breathes life into a backdrop of wood mills and century old farms

Eugene, a crossroads town, where people from all over bring with them their hopes and dreams and make a serious attempt to flesh them out. On a summer day, one can spot 50-100 people with backpacks, traveling the West, interluding in Eugene; camping by the river, in alleys, or on the couches or floors of friends, new or old.

Across the Willamette River is Springfield, where Matt Groening, creator of the "Simpsons" went to High School. Springfield, unified within it's own history, blue collar working class; 9-5 they'll expect of You there. Together the two cities make up the 2nd largest urban area in Oregon.

O When starting out on this one 2 week bicycle/camping trip in late September, before I even got as far as Marcola, I wrecked on my bike. A scraped bloody elbow, a big chunk of skin roadburned off the heel of my right hand. My hand kept bleeding for three hours.... I kept licking it clean and spitting out the blood as I continued to ride. It is in all of our experiences to wipe out at one time or another in what we're doing, to get right back up and continue on our way nonetheless

O After months of wondering about the small towns I saw in my Oregon Road Atlas book, I set out to take a look at them, mostly the ones not along the interstate. I was in search of an archtypal Oregon town, which perhaps only exists in my imagination.

Sigh.... it seems that whenever a town gets over a certain size, say 500-750 souls, the chain stores move in; so it was only in the least populated off the main road towns that seemed to retain a distinct Oregonianess.

The town which seemed closest to an archtypal Oregon town was Scio. Old buildings kept up, Mom and Pop stores, a park with a plaque that said it was run by volunteers, active older folks and wholesome looking younger folks. Late afternoon at the grocery store, a bunch on teenage guys were standing around. One of them called out to two girls who were walking by, "Do either of You have a dollar?" One of the girls replied, "No,

Glenwood

but I can get one, what do you need it for?"

O Early Sunday morning, the first town I came to was Estcada, where I found an open restaurant serving coffee. A middle aged woman sitting in a booth with her son greeted the people who came in with "How Y'all doing?" in a Southern accent, but she talked with them in a regular Oregon accent.

A vibrant excited woman in her mid 20's came in with a girlfriend of hers. People gathered around her table sharing in her excitement. Overhearing the conversation I gathered she was getting married this same day. One woman there asked her what jewelry she was going to wear. She answered, "Only the earrings my Grandfather gave to my Grandmother on their first wedding anniversary".

O Of all the places I rode through on the bicycle trip, the place I would most like to stay for a while was the dismal vibed city/town of Astoria, the oldest American settlement on the West Coast, where American fur trappers built a camp in 1810. By West Coast standards it is old, with ruins, streets and streets of historical buildings and houses. There is an ordinariness there that permeates the dampness.

O At a weekday yard sale along a country road, I was greeted by barking dogs who quieted up when I petted them. A melancholy woman with half her face burned and scarred from a fire in her past tried to keep the unburned side of her face turned toward me. She seemed vulnerable and a little scared. I looked around the tables cluttered with all sorts of leftover possesions, searching for books of interest to me. I purchased 6 old postcards with scenes of Eskimos and space travel.

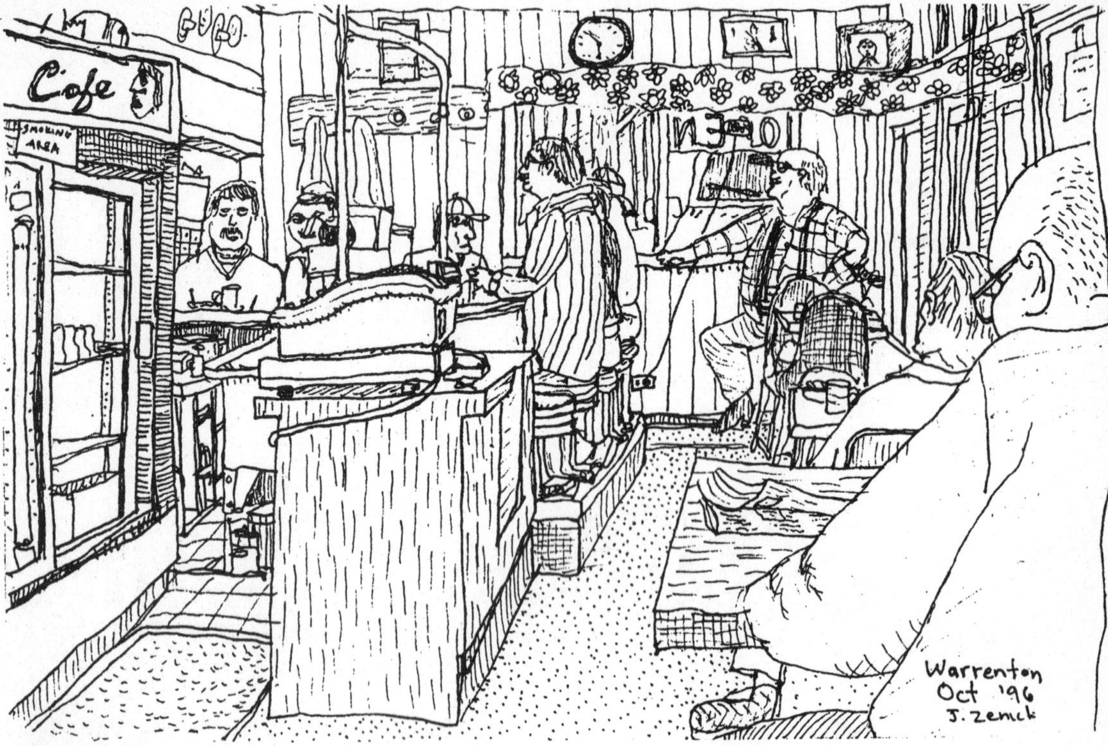
Cafe
SMOKING AREA
OPEN
Warrenton
Oct '96
J. Zenick

Taking a rest along the side of the road near the community of Goble by the Columbia River, I got in a conversation and walked down to the river with a saddened looking guy, same age as me, who poured out his troubles about a judge ordering him to sell his land (which he and his ex-wife had bought from his Dad), where he had lived since he was 8. He was to split the money he got from the land with his ex-wife. There must be a way I can keep my land... but how? he wondered.

Along the river he pointed out a decaying dock where gravel had been loaded onto ships 20 years ago. He pointed out rocks along the shore of the river which he had been scampering over since he was a kid.

At a pulloff by some cliffs overlooking the Columbia, I saw a man setting up some sort of small radar. He was traveling in a beat-up Toyota pick-up truck with a camper on the back and pro-environment bumper stickers on the bumpers.

I rode up to him and asked him what he was up to. He was checking out frequencies and points of receptivity where Sea Lions that were going to have radio transmitter placed in their ears migrated past. He was part of a project team who hoped to trace the yearly migration of the Sea Lions. He rattled on about these creatures, his love for them evident in his voice.

When I reached the Pacific Coast I was drenched by 5 days and nights of rain till I crossed the Coast Range back into the Willamette Valley, heading East at Newport.

Riding along the Coast in the rain, three times I crossed paths with Thomas (pronounced Toe-maas), a German who had bicycled from Montreal and was on his way to San Francisco. It was comical keeping running into him, braving the rain and completely drenched like I was.

With a bivi-sack and an Army tarp I mananged to keep reasonably dry while camping in the rain. A person makes due with the tools they are given. Our ability to tolerate hardships has it's pluses and minuses...

KID *Medusa's* VERY OWN COCKTAIL:

the SWEETIE

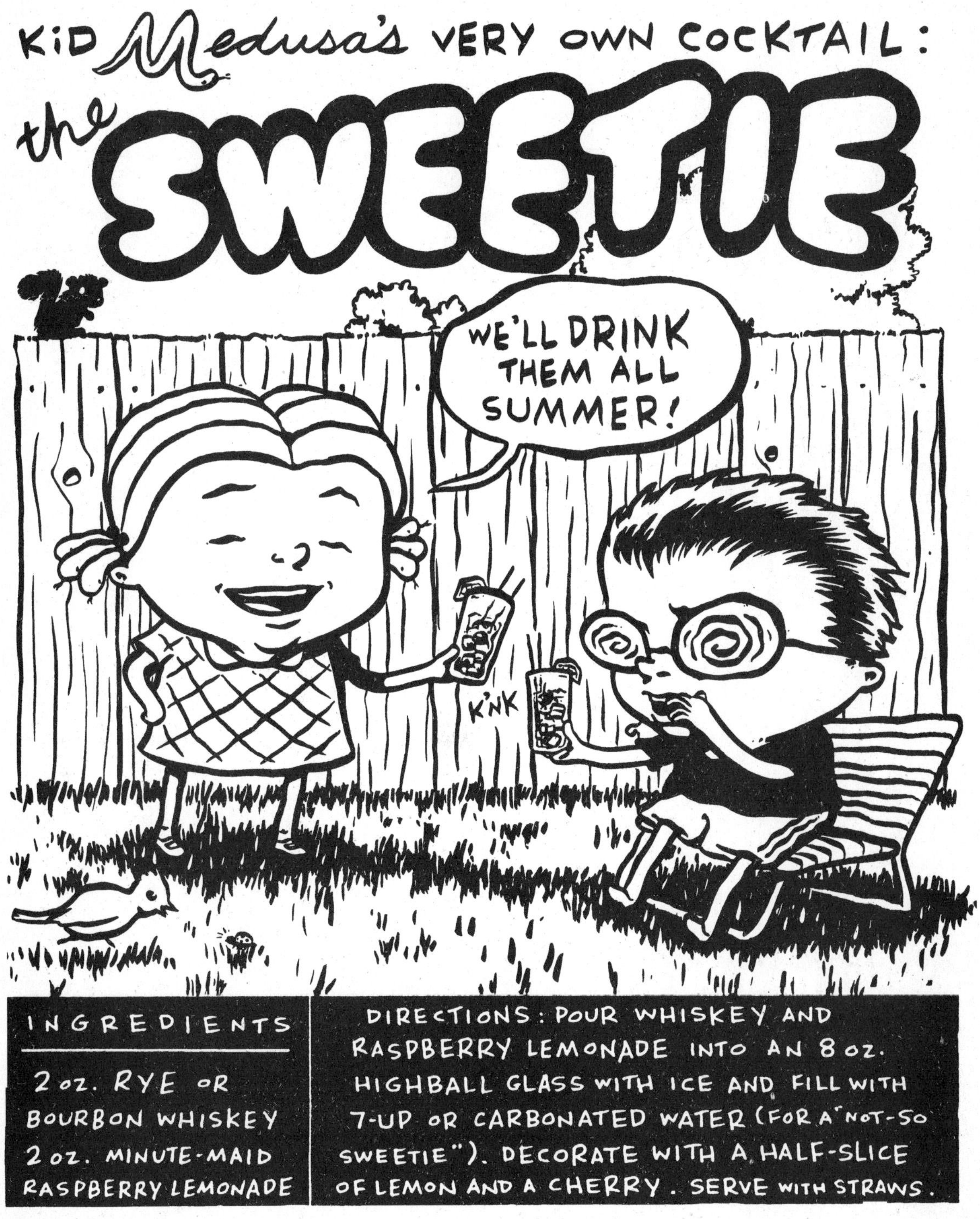
WE'LL DRINK THEM ALL SUMMER!
K'NK

INGREDIENTS

2 oz. RYE or BOURBON WHISKEY
2 oz. MINUTE-MAID RASPBERRY LEMONADE

DIRECTIONS: POUR WHISKEY AND RASPBERRY LEMONADE INTO AN 8 oz. HIGHBALL GLASS WITH ICE AND FILL WITH 7-UP OR CARBONATED WATER (FOR A "NOT-SO SWEETIE"). DECORATE WITH A HALF-SLICE OF LEMON AND A CHERRY. SERVE WITH STRAWS.

THE DISASTER

By Alan Hunt

"If I ever get a girlfriend," I once said, half-jokingly, to a room-mate: "You know that the first thing that I'm going to do is clean up that bathroom."

My two room-mates and I share the washroom with a family of five 'Potato Bugs'. Nobody really seems to mind them, but I thought that it was only fair to warn them:

If I ever get a girlfriend, you guys are outta' here!

One day, last Autumn, I thought that I might have been on the verge of a relationship and, in honour of this, I went downstairs and scrubbed, scrubbed, SCRUBBED...

I was amazed by how dirty everything really was, and, of course, I swore to keep it clean from that day forward.

It feels good to clean!

However, I still didn't have the heart to get rid of the 'Potato Bugs'-- call it misplaced empathy I guess...

You're alright.

The whole 'Girlfriend' thing turned out to be a false alarm and I stopped caring about the condition of the Bathroom.

After discovering a mouse in the garbage my room-mate went on a caulking Rampage; filling in cracks and fissures anywhere he could.

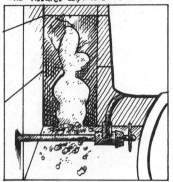

The other day I was sitting on the toilet when I noticed that all around me lay the upturned corpses of 'Potato Bugs'-- a Kleenex shoved into their home at the base of the door-frame.

I knew that it was inevitable but never-the-less I felt mad-- mad at my room-mate for taking the decision out of my hands, and at myself for not **really** caring.

May, 1997.

FRIENDS & FAMILY

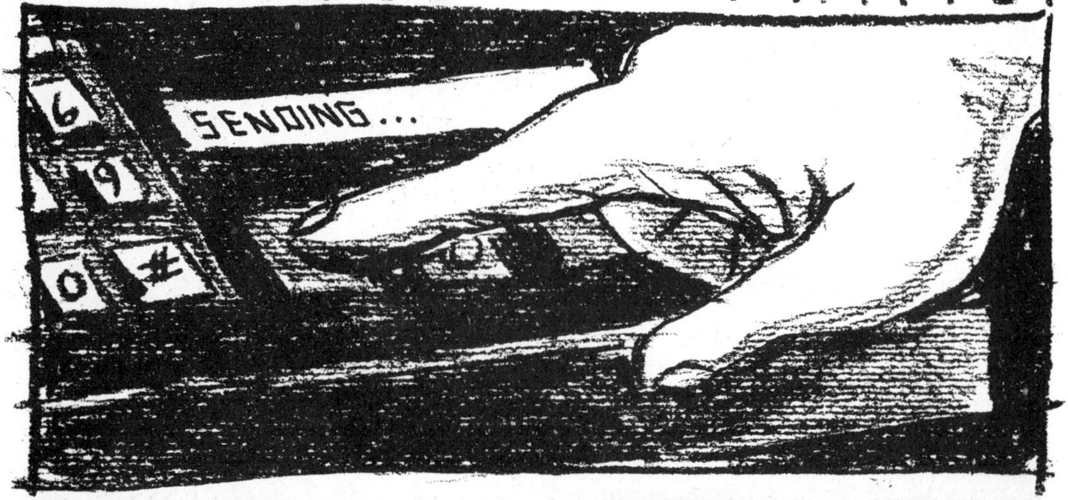
SENDING...

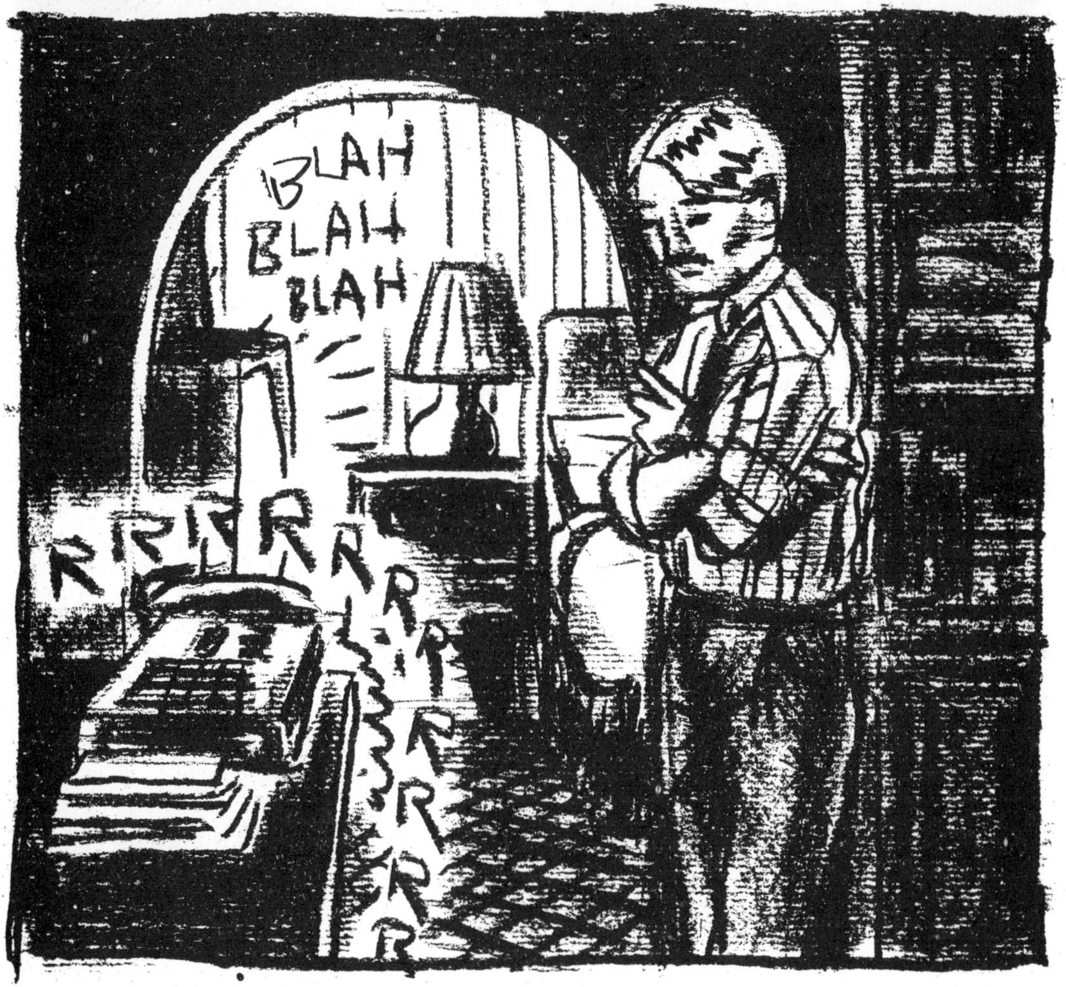
BLAH
BLAH
BLAH
RRRRRRRRRRRRR

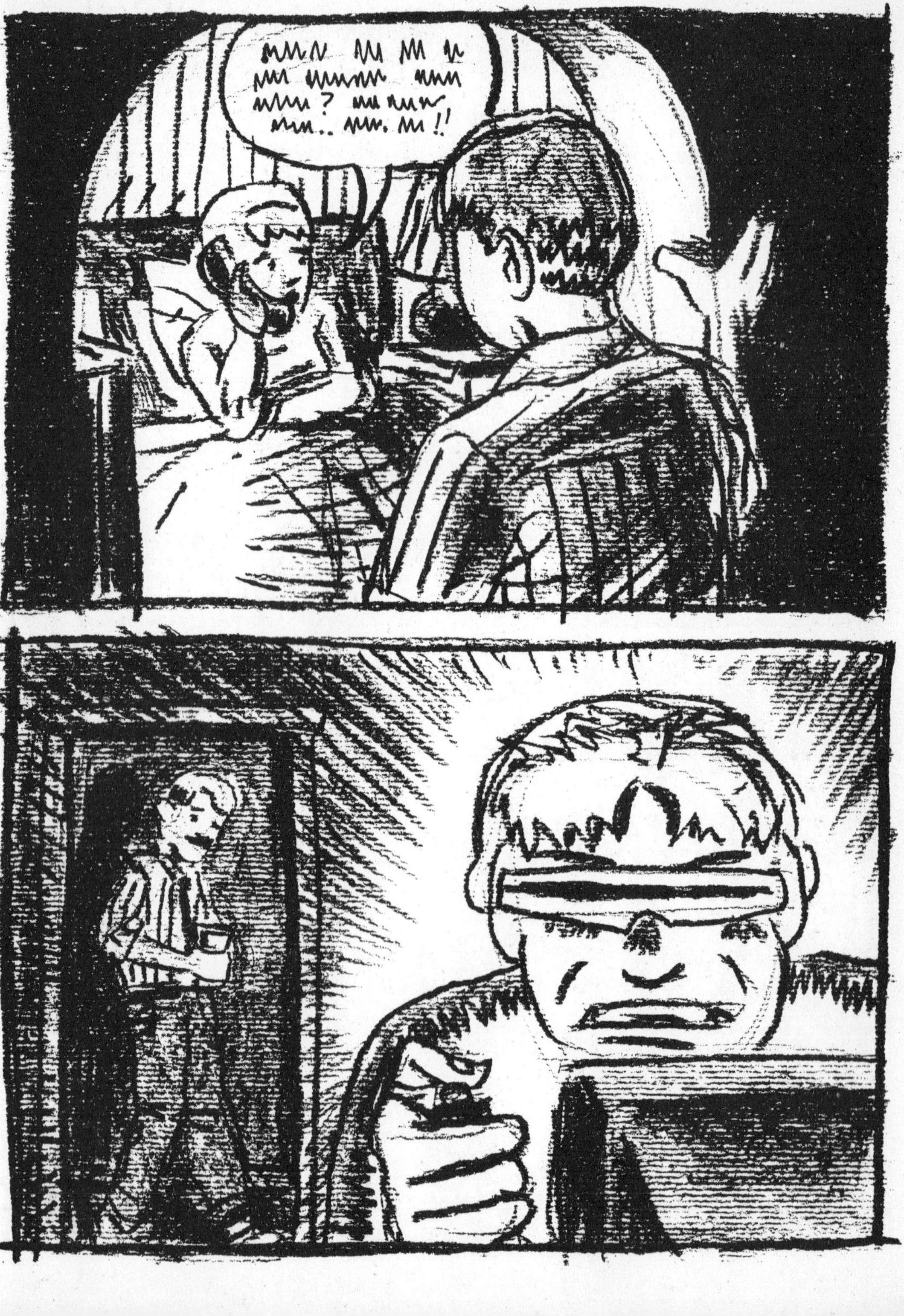

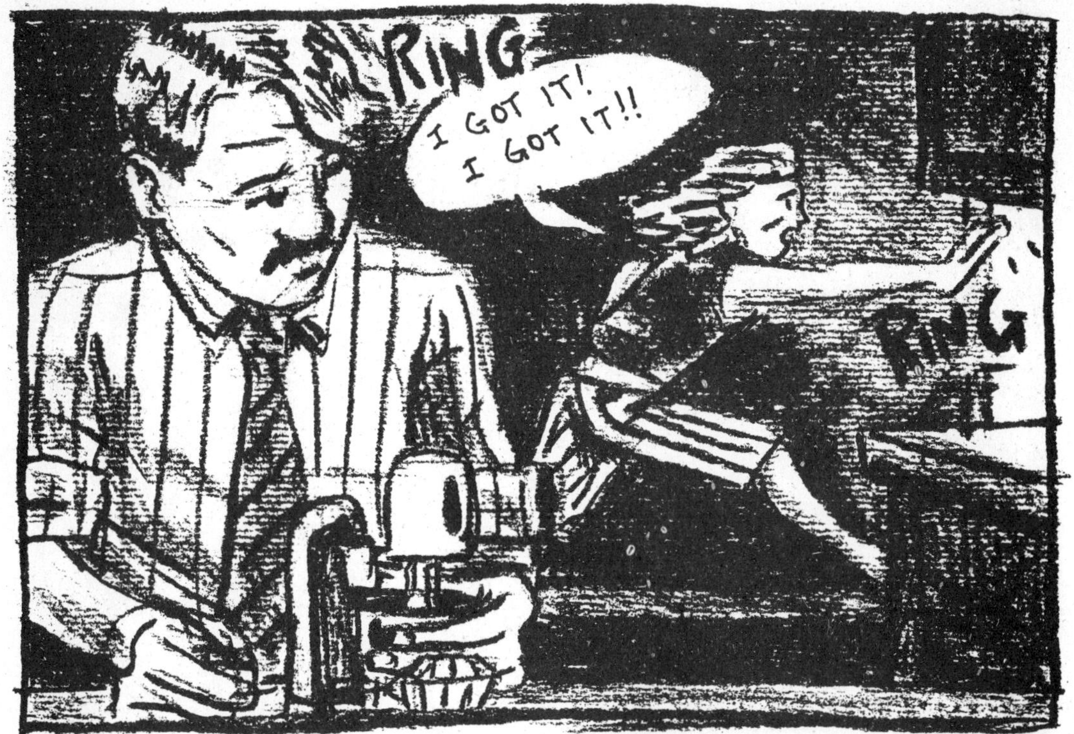
RING
I GOT IT! I GOT IT!!
RING

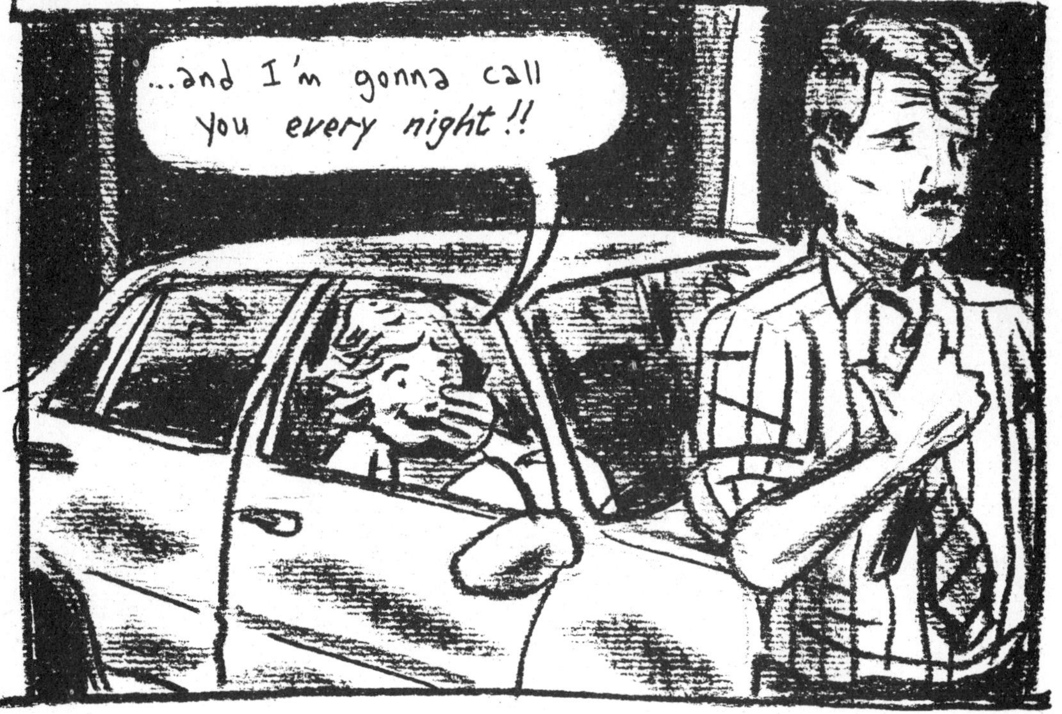
...and I'm gonna call you *every night*!!

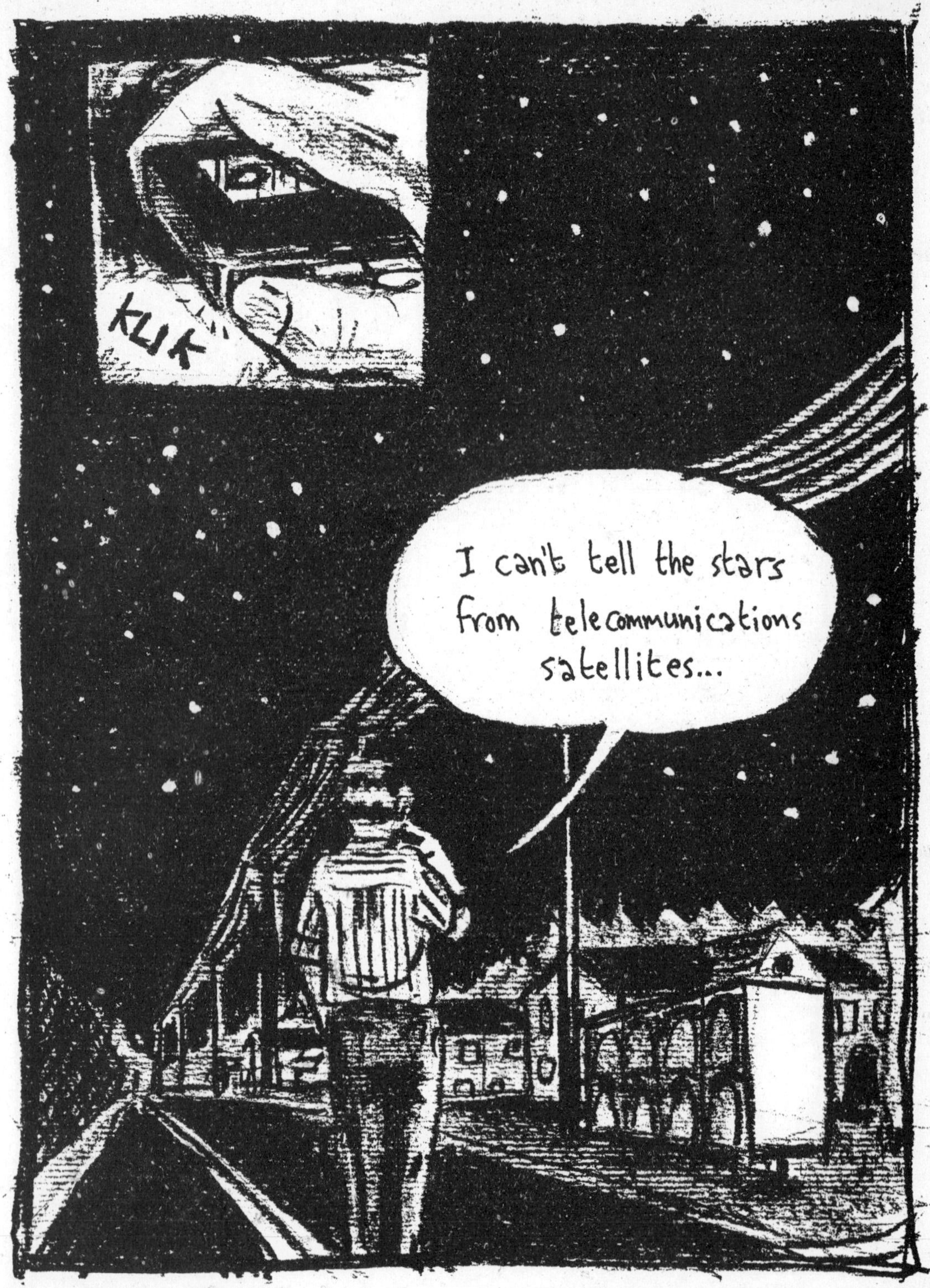
KLIK
I can't tell the stars from telecommunications satellites...

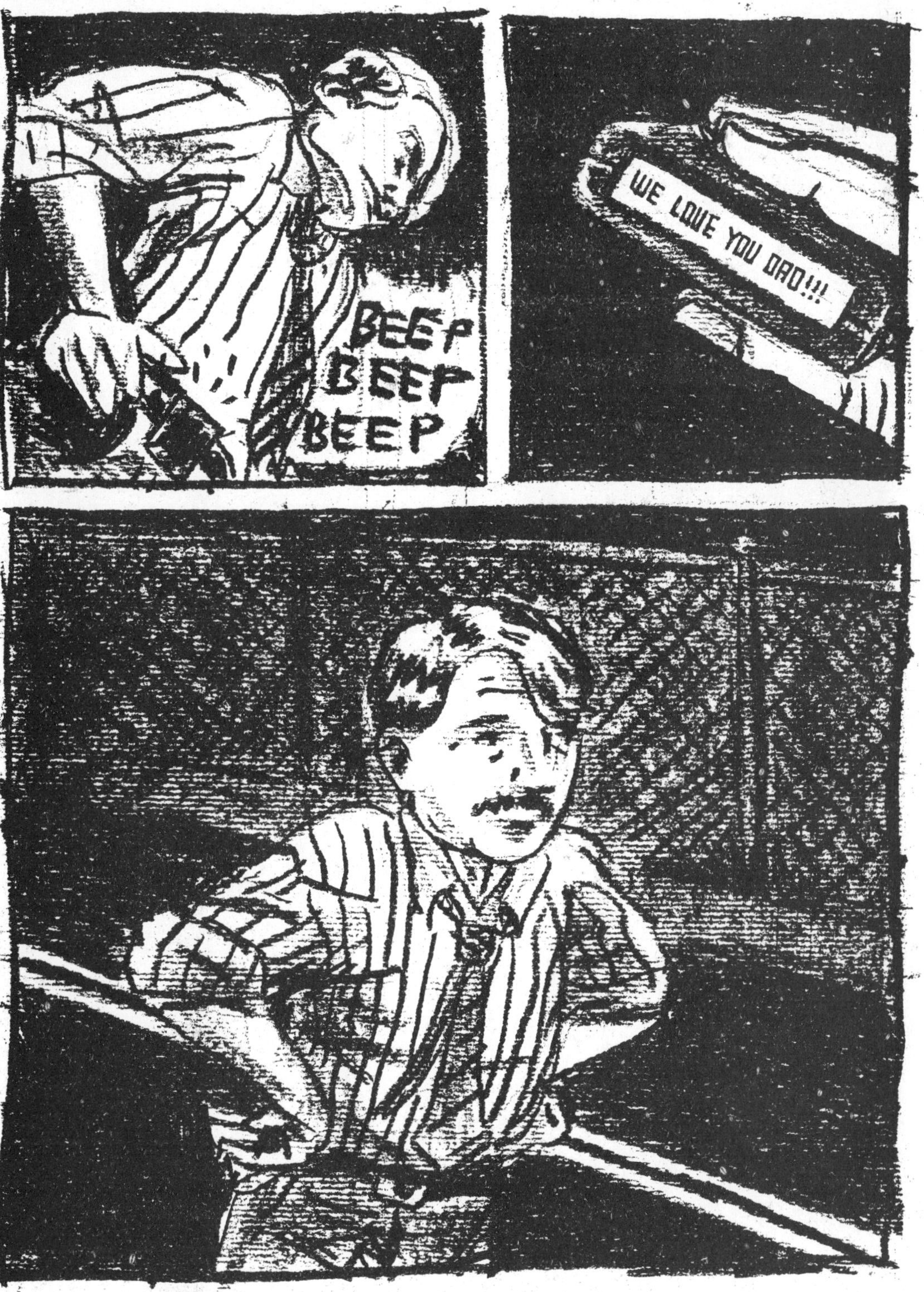
BEEP
BEEP
BEEP
WE LOVE YOU DAD!!!

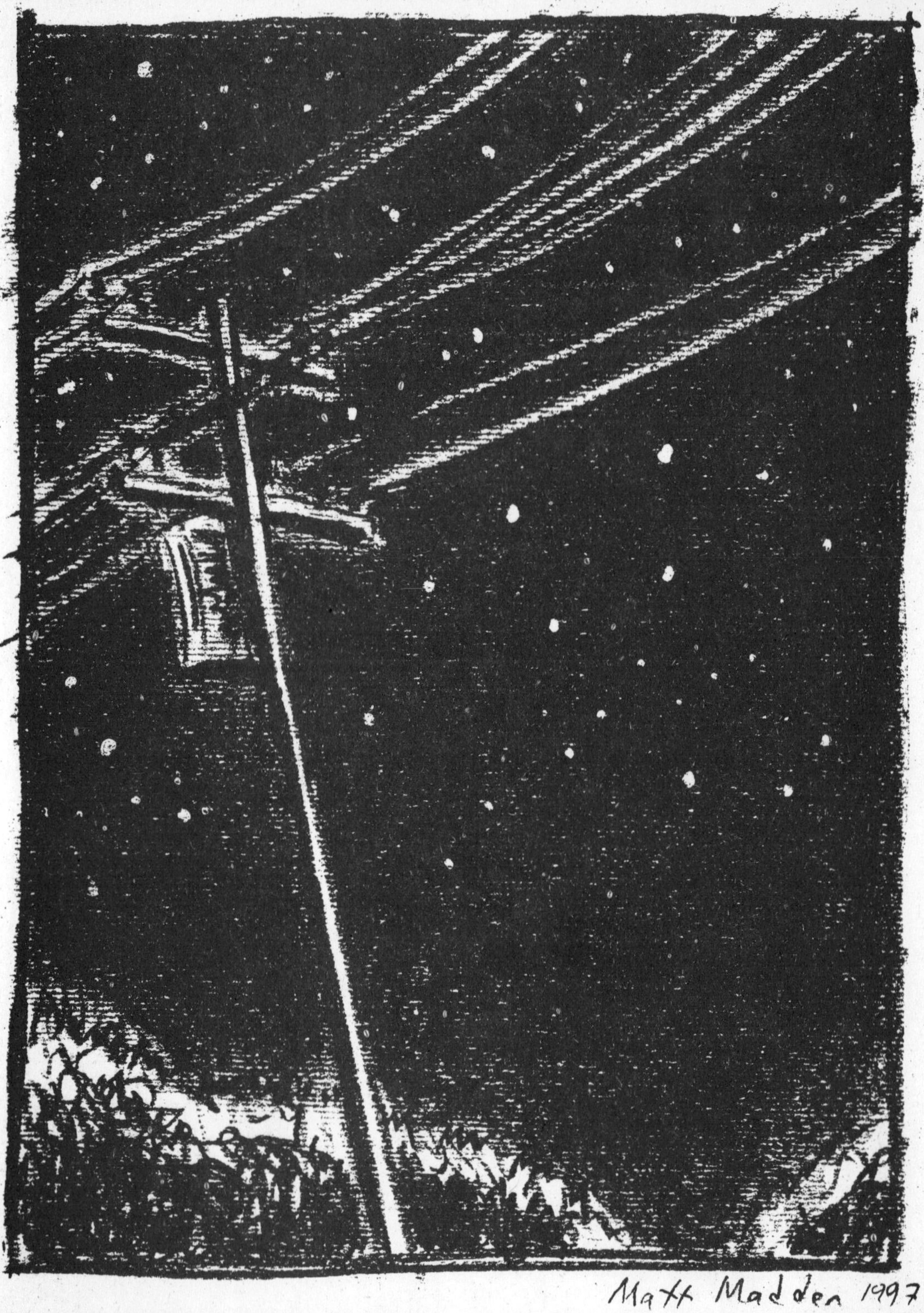

Matt Madden 1997